MUSICAL COMPOSITION

A SHORT TREATISE FOR STUDENTS

BY

CHARLES VILLIERS STANFORD

Copyright © 2018 Read Books Ltd.
This book is copyright and may not be
reproduced or copied in any way without
the express permission of the publisher in writing

British Library Cataloguing-in-Publication Data
A catalogue record for this book is available from
the British Library

PREFATORY NOTE

THIS little treatise does not pretend to do more than touch the fringe of a great subject. It only attempts to give such advice as a master might find useful in teaching (or rather in controlling) a student of composition; and it is, to some extent, a résumé of the experience of twenty-five years in watching and criticising the efforts of many young men, some of whom have risen, and some of whom are rising, to eminence in their craft. The author has not (as is usually the case) to express his obligation to any authorities for help or assistance in its making, for he unfortunately knows of no modern treatise which would have suited his purpose. Composers are usually reticent as to their methods and experiences, probably because they are too much immersed in creative work to analyse the means which enabled them to write it. To do so with thoroughness would fill volumes, probably so thick that no one would wade through their contents, and if they are good composers they are better employed in inventing good music. But he has to put on record a very deep sense of gratitude to a numerous and many-sided body of pupils who, in learning from him, have taught him how to teach, and by their unvarying loyalty and keen endeavour have

PREFATORY NOTE

minimised the anxiety and magnified the interest of his labours on their behalf. Many of them will recognise old friends in the pages of this book, and it is in the hope that these old friends may make new acquaintances, and be of some service to them, that it has been allowed to venture into print.

April, 1911.

IN GRATEFUL MEMORY

OF

THE MASTERS WHO TAUGHT ME

CONTENTS

CHAPTER		PAGE
I.	Introductory	1
II.	Technique	6
III.	Rhythm	23
IV.	Melodies and their Simple Treatment	33
V.	The Complex Treatment of Melodies. Variation	49
VI.	Form	74
VII.	Colour	95
VIII.	The Treatment of Voices	127
IX.	Extraneous Influences in Instrumental Music	155
X.	Danger Signals	165

CHAPTER I

INTRODUCTORY

THE composition of music is no more an exact science than the painting of a picture. No rules can be laid down for it, no canons save those of beauty can be applied to it; and as invention, without which it cannot exist, may be said to be infinite, so there are no fixed bounds to its capabilities. Any treatise upon composition, therefore, can only consist of advice and criticism chiefly directed to what concerns taste and sense of proportion. To tell a student how to write music is an impossible absurdity. The only province of a teacher is to criticise it when written, or to make suggestions as to its form or length, or as to the instruments or voices for which it should be designed. He can thus keep impatience within bounds when invention is outpacing experience, and develop by sure, if sometimes necessarily slow, means the experience to equal the invention. For the rest his functions must be what those of this treatise must be, mainly to give hints as to what to avoid, leaving the constructive element to the pupil's own initiative.

It is not possible to discuss composition without to some extent touching upon other branches of musical study which form an integral part of its proper presentiment, such as Counterpoint, Harmony, Rhythm, Modulation, Form, individual and collective treatment of instruments and voices; for there is no short cut to mastery. The house cannot stand if it is built upon insecure foundations, and its security depends upon a knowledge of technique which involves the hardest and at times the driest drudgery. It is often disheartening, often apparently superfluous, but the enthusiasm which is not strong enough to face the irksome training and lasting enough to see it through to a finish had better be allowed to die out. In this respect the history of all arts is the same. In painting and sculpture, it is the mastery of drawing, perspective and anatomy: in architecture, of construction: in literature and poetry, of grammar: in music, of counterpoint, harmony and form. The lack of technical knowledge in an architect may lead to loss of human life. In the other arts it as certainly means shortness of existence to the creations of the half-equipped artist. Technique is of no use without invention, invention is of no use without technique. One is the servant, the other the master; but the mastery is gained by having complete control of the servant.

It is, moreover, of the highest importance that the training of technique should be as strict as that the supervision of composition should be elastic. The application of technical criticism to inventive work is a most dangerous expedient. It tends (as Brahms forcibly put it) to the manufacture of Philistines on the one hand, and of red Revolutionaries on the other. If the technical equipment of the composer is complete, it is unnecessary; if it is incomplete, technical deficiencies in his composition should be criticised as such,

INTRODUCTORY

and should be kept wholly distinct from questions of taste. A composer who has full knowledge of his technique, and can play about with a canon or fugue, has got to a point where he can utilise his knowledge to make experiments. A man who knows he is writing consecutive fifths can write them if he is convinced of their appropriateness, and can convince the hearer of their beauty, without being pulled up by the old formula of infringement of rule; for in composition *per se* there is no rule save that of beauty, and no standard save that of taste. It is only the composer who knows the rules of the game, and the why and wherefore of those rules, who can understand when and how to break them.

On the other hand, teachers often overlook the natural tendency of a young and ardent inventive brain to chafe under advice which at the moment seems merely formal, irksome and dry. This impatience of temperament cannot be curbed merely by dogmatic insistence upon the rules themselves; it can only be moulded and brought into line by the sympathetic method of explaining why these rules were laid down and by clearly showing their origin. In counterpoint, for example, a beginner who is conversant with the developments of modern music cannot be expected to understand a rule which "forbids" a skip from 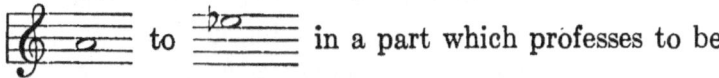 a melody written to fit another melody. But when it is explained to him that this rule was made in the early times for music written for the unaccompanied human voice, an instrument which possesses no mechanical means of hitting a note as the pianoforte has, and which therefore finds great difficulty in producing diminished and augmented intervals with accurate intonation, he will begin at once to appreciate that such a rule is founded, not for the purpose of annoying students or laying traps for beginners, or of providing materials for examination papers, but on the principles of common sense. It is a rule only in the same sense that it is laid down that the student of orchestration should abstain from writing [musical notation] for the violin, or putting on paper arpeggios for stringed instruments which are technically impossible to play. Such explanations of the origin of rules will appeal to the sympathy of the student, when a mere insistence upon the rule as a rule will only irritate him.

Music itself has grown from the simplest beginnings through their gradual development; if the student begins his career by trying to write music in the style of the later Beethoven, he will be as great a monstrosity as a pianist who attempted to play Liszt before he knew his five-finger exercises. As the executive artist has to develop his muscles slowly and gradually without straining them, so the creative artist has to develop his brain. Any impatient interference with natural process and progress will inevitably result in disaster. Robert Schumann in his anxiety to make himself too speedily a first-rate pianist irretrievably damaged his third finger; a young composer in a hurry can do precisely similar harm to the machine which makes his music for him, his brain. All the music which has survived the ravages of time has been

INTRODUCTORY

inherently logical, it states its premisses and evolves its conclusions. Music which begins with conclusions and omits premisses is useless and lifeless from its birth.

It will be understood, therefore, that in this treatise the word "rule" is not to be taken as synonymous with "the laws of the Medes and Persians"; that it deals rather with advice and suggestion than with dogmatic orders; that it has primarily to do with taste, and the moulding of good taste; and that it premises that the paradise to be obtained is that of beauty, and the hell to be avoided is that of ugliness.

CHAPTER II

TECHNIQUE

IT would appear to be a platitude to state that the first step in musical composition is the ability to write one note after another, and to arrange the succession of notes in such a way as to produce an intelligible and agreeable sound. The result of this process is what is known as melody. The first training for a student should be in the direction of developing his power of writing these successions of notes with ease and fluency; the second of combining them with other successions of notes which will result both in giving richness to the original and in providing a second subsidiary melody. The initial training should be, therefore, horizontal and not perpendicular. Mere combinations of notes, in themselves sounding well, but without logical connection with their successors, are useless as music. The simultaneous presentation of two melodies which fit each other is at once a musical invention; and when a third and a fourth melody is added to the combinations, the result is what is called harmony. To speak of studying harmony and counterpoint is, therefore, to put the cart before the horse. It is counterpoint which develops harmony, and there is no such boundary-wall between the two studies as most students imagine.

TECHNIQUE

Harmony which results from the well-written combination of melodies will always be interesting both as a whole and in its separate parts; but an exercise in harmony written before the student has practised melodic writing, will (unless he has exceptional melodic intuition) be dry even if it is technically correct. If a student begins by thinking of chords, no matter how agreeable they may be to the ear, his first attempts to write a composition will infallibly be in blocks of chords; the theme, even if it is lucky enough to run smoothly of itself, will be hampered by the inability of its companions to do the same. The simplest instance of this principle is to give a correct harmonisation in four parts of the scale of F major, with which, from a harmony point of view, no fault can be found, but which is as dull and uninteresting as it can well be:

No. 1.

and to compare it with a two-part contrapuntal combination on the same scale:

No. 2.

which, although it has no rich chords, is far more

interesting to listen to. Moreover, the melody which accompanies the scale becomes at once a satisfying bass, which compares most favourably with the stilted and halting bass of No. 1.

A mind which is trained to write a melody to a melody would never be satisfied with the four repeated F's in the alto part of No. 1, or with the limited range of the tenor part.

By adding a third melodic part in the alto, the gradual appearance of harmony will become obvious:

and a fourth melodic part in the tenor will make the phrase as complete as the harmony example, but far more satisfactory to the ear and grateful to the voice:

or, in slightly more ornamental form:

These examples are sufficient in themselves to show the immense advantage which counterpoint has over harmony as an initial training. The chords form themselves naturally without interfering with the vocal progressions, and only need harmony lessons to explain their significance when read perpendicularly. To begin technical training with harmony gives rise also to a habit in a beginner, which it is most difficult to eradicate when he embarks on composition, the habit of harmonising every note of the melody and keeping every part hard at work *without rests*. The usefulness of rests is one of the essentials of composition. A piece of music has to breathe like a human being; the rests are the breathing places. The absence of them invariably results in stodginess and monotony. Again, counterpoint teaches economy of material, one of the most important (and most frequently neglected) requirements of the composer. It does so by the suggestions of chords which are not actually complete, and by training the mind to utilise suggestion as a necessary contrast to defined richness of chord combination. An excellent instance of the result of this system is to be found in the last movement of the Ninth Symphony of Beethoven, where the theme is first presented without any combination at all, and is repeated with gradually enriched surroundings. Of this example and of the Prometheus Variations (used also in the finale of the Eroica Symphony) mention will be made later. The first principle to be laid down is, therefore, to **study counterpoint first, and through counterpoint to master harmony.**

It is not necessary to remind a student of musical history that this was the process by which were trained all the great masters from Palestrina down to Wagner and Brahms.

The policy of putting harmony before counterpoint is of comparatively recent growth; the growth has unfortunately overrun a great deal of low-lying land, and it is easy enough to note where it flourishes from the results of its miasma. To the advanced modern student it may be interesting to point out that such works as the *Meistersinger, Parsifal,* and the *German Requiem* did not grow on this tainted soil; nor, to go to the other extreme of style, did the waltzes of Johann Strauss.

The second principle is that the **study of counterpoint, if it is to be of real value, must be strict.** It has recently become the fashion to speak of counterpoint as if it were divided into two branches, strict and free. There is no such thing as free counterpoint from the standpoint of technical study. It is only a pedantic name for composition. All musical works are in free counterpoint, and the use of this quasi-scholastic title at once suggests the introduction of handcuffs and shackles into the free domain of creative invention. It would be as sensible to speak of the Pentonville Hotel or the Wormwood Scrubbs Boarding House. The thorough knowledge and grasp of strict counterpoint is all that is necessary in that department of study. If the term free counterpoint means that the student may use less trammelled rules, take liberties, and use licences which strict counterpoint does not allow, he is weakening the very process by which his musical strength is built up. He will be pretending to develop his muscles with dumb-bells from which the weight has been extracted; the result will be a sham, and his control over his workmanship will be superficial and unsound. The composer who trusts to it will fail at a crisis, and will be the first to regret, perhaps too late, the easy path which he believed to be a short cut to efficiency. The intangible nature of musical sounds makes it more difficult for a student to appreciate the importance of strict training. A sculptor who attempted to model a figure without a complete grasp of human anatomy would be found out at once by the first medical student who saw his work. Hogarth has immortalised the result of ignorance of perspective. The building of Forth Bridges is not entrusted to engineers who are insufficiently grounded in applied mathematics, nor to contractors who cannot guarantee the absence of flaws in their material. A composer produces a work which cannot be felt as a statue, or seen as a picture, or tested for strain and stress as a bridge; it appeals through the ear alone, and is, therefore, more difficult to test for value and soundness; but the canons for art, whether ocular or auricular, are the same in all respects, and cannot be infringed without sooner or later involving disaster to the work and its inventor. The study of strict counterpoint, then, is the only method of enabling the brain to cope with the difficulties which waylay invention.

What is strict counterpoint? The best way of finding an answer to that highly important question is to investigate history and see what kind of strict counterpoint was the main study of the great masters of the past, whose works have best withstood the inroads of time. Let us take for our inquiry such names as Palestrina, Purcell, Bach, Handel, Haydn, Mozart, Beethoven, Wagner and Brahms. Every one of these masters was brought up upon what is called modal counterpoint, at once the most interesting and the most severe form of the study. [The printed contrapuntal studies of Beethoven with Haydn are most instructive in this respect.] Its main general features, and the side-issues which it involves, require a section to themselves.

STRICT MODAL COUNTERPOINT.

The musician whose instrument is the pianoforte or organ starts with the great drawback that his ear is accustomed to hear every note in the scale except the octave slightly out of tune. If he is suddenly summoned to examine and report upon a violinist, he will be entirely incapable of saying with accuracy whether the player possesses the sense of pure intonation; intervals which to him are quite satisfactory he will discover to his surprise to be quite the reverse to an expert violin player; and he will find that it is necessary for him to begin all over again, and to school his ear to the pure scale. A musician who has begun his career by learning a stringed instrument will find no such difficulty; but to one who has absorbed the compromise known as "equal temperament," it will come as something of a shock to discover that his idea of the scale is confined to keyed instruments, and that in the orchestra and in voices it has no place. For him Palestrina and all the early masters of unaccompanied vocal music are a sealed book. He may like the sounds they produce, but he does not know why. He may wonder at the silken quality of a string quartet, but he will not know the reason which underlies it. He may be surprised that chords (*e.g.* in Wagner), which sound crude on his piano, lose all their roughness in the orchestra, but he cannot analyse the cause. For the composer, therefore, it is an absolute necessity that he should **study the pure scale and write in it.** The basis of the pure scale is that diatonic semitones are a fixed interval, and tones changeable. There is a greater tone and a lesser tone. In the pure scale of C the interval (*a*) is slightly wider than the interval (*b*). If the interval (*a*) were in perfect intonation, and the same distance were to be applied to (*b*), the result would be a major third which was too wide, and the diatonic semitone would be too small to satisfy the ear. These greater and lesser tones are alternative in the scale.

14   MUSICAL COMPOSITION

If < = the greater tone and > = the lesser tone, the pure scale of C will be constituted thus:

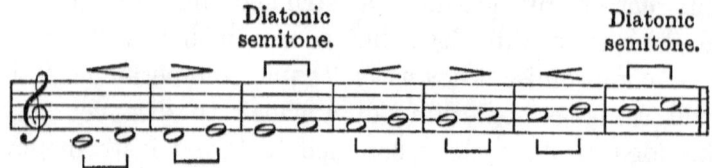

(The student is recommended to test this scale on a violin.)

The ratios of the intervals have been calculated out, and are as follows:

Diatonic semitone	$\frac{16}{15}$
Lesser tone	$\frac{10}{9}$
Greater tone	$\frac{9}{8}$
Major third	$\frac{5}{4}$
Perfect fourth	$\frac{4}{3}$
Perfect fifth	$\frac{3}{2}$
Major sixth	$\frac{5}{3}$
Major seventh	$\frac{15}{8}$
Octave	$\frac{2}{1}$

These can easily be verified on the violin with the help of a yard measure,

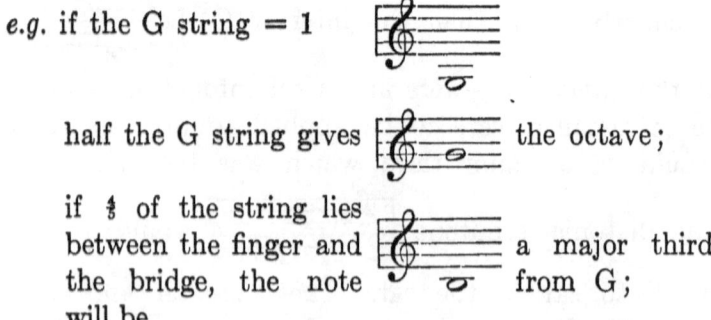

e.g. if the G string = 1

half the G string gives   the octave;

if ⅘ of the string lies between the finger and the bridge, the note will be   a major third from G;

TECHNIQUE

if ¾ of the string lies
between the finger and
the bridge, the note
will be ♩ a perfect fourth from G;

and so on throughout the scale.

When harmonies are added to the notes of the scale of C, one note has to be liable to change and is termed "mutable." This note is D, the second degree, which must be the lesser tone from C ($\frac{9}{10}$) in order to combine with F and A (the supertonic triad), and the greater tone from C ($\frac{8}{9}$) in order to combine with G. This can be tested arithmetically by calculating the interval from C to F ($\frac{3}{4}$), the perfect fifth from D to A ($\frac{2}{3}$), and the major third from F to A ($\frac{4}{5}$), which will show that to make the chord ♩ perfectly in tune, the interval from C to D must be $\frac{9}{10}$, and from D to E $\frac{8}{9}$. Similar investigation will show that to combine with G, D must be a greater tone ($\frac{8}{9}$) from C in order to make a perfect fourth ($\frac{3}{4}$) with G.

The minor scale is constituted thus:

The ratios of these intervals are as follows:

Lesser tone . . . . $\frac{9}{10}$
Greater tone . . . . $\frac{8}{9}$
Minor third . . . . $\frac{5}{6}$
Perfect fourth . . . . $\frac{3}{4}$

Perfect fifth . . . . $\frac{2}{3}$
Minor sixth . . . . $\frac{5}{8}$
Minor seventh . . . . $\frac{9}{16}$
Octave . . . . $\frac{1}{2}$

When harmonies are added to this scale, two notes are mutable, B, the second degree, and G, the seventh degree. B must be the lesser tone from A to combine with D, and G must be the lesser tone from F to combine with B and D [notation]. On the other hand, B must be the greater tone from A to combine with E, and G must be the greater tone from F to combine with B and E [notation]. This can be similarly tested by applying the ratios for a minor third (B to D), minor sixth (B to G), and perfect fourth (D to G), in the first case; and by applying them for a perfect fourth (B to E), minor sixth (B to G), and minor third (E to G), in the second case.

The student will soon grasp the reason for mutable notes, either by experimenting himself on a violin or by getting a violinist to show him the modifications necessary in the stopping in order to make the intervals perfectly in tune, and by comparing the result (with the greatest possible accuracy of ear) with the same combinations on the pianoforte; and he can, if arithmetically inclined, work out the same results by calculating the ratios of the intervals in figures. The best system is to do both; and it becomes a study of great interest to find that the mathematical results

TECHNIQUE

coincide absolutely with the practical. [To get the ratio of a given interval from the bass, multiply the fractions, *e.g.* to calculate the ratio of the interval C to E multiply $\frac{9}{8}$ (the greater tone) by $\frac{10}{9}$ (the lesser tone), result $\frac{5}{4}$ (a major third). To get the difference between any two intervals divide the higher by the lower, *e.g.* to calculate the ratio of G to B divide $\frac{10}{9}$ by $\frac{8}{9}$, result $\frac{5}{4}$ (a major third).]

The ear will soon begin to "think" in the pure scale, and as soon as it does the brain will invent music in the pure scale. But just as a would-be linguist cannot freely talk in a foreign language until he is able to think in it also, so a composer cannot write in the pure scale until he thinks in it.

The student of some interesting modern developments will also speedily discover that the adoption of the so-called whole-tone scale as a basis of music is, except upon a keyed instrument tuned to the compromise of equal temperament, unnatural and impossible. No player upon a stringed instrument can play the scale of whole tones and arrive at an octave which is in tune with the starting note, unless he deliberately changes one of the notes on the road, and alters it while playing it. The obvious result of the application of the whole-tone scale to an orchestra or a string quartet would be to force them to adopt the equal temperament of the pianoforte, and to play every interval except the octave out of tune. When this modification had taken hold, all music written in the pure scale would be distorted and destroyed, unless string players were to face the practically impossible drudgery of studying both the equal temperament and the pure scale from the start, and were able to tackle either form at a moment's notice. A thorough knowledge of the natural genesis of the scale of western nations will be the best antidote to fads founded upon ignorance of it. It is a curious commentary upon this question that Wagner, in the opening of the third act of *Tristan* (bars 6 to 10), experimented with the whole-tone scale, and drew his pen through it, as was to be expected from a composer whose every work proves the writer to have had the pure scale inbred in him. A student will find it interesting to test the whole-tone scale on the arithmetical formulas given above.

Modal counterpoint possesses also another great attraction to the student. Instead of two scales in which to write, he has six: every one of them different in constitution (that is, in the succession of tones and semitones). He has, therefore, at his command three times the variety of the contrapuntist who bases himself solely on the ordinary major and minor scales. Every one of these modes has its own colour and characteristics (as the student of folk-song or of early madrigals well knows), and the range of suggestiveness is proportionately greater. The difficulty which has first to be faced in modal writing is to accustom the ear to grasp that the last note of those modes which do not correspond to our major and minor scales is really the final. A cadence in the Mixo-Lydian mode (G to G with F natural) will to the tyro sound like ending in the dominant; the cadence in the Lydian (F to F) like ending in the subdominant. A reference to the slow movement in the Lydian mode of Beethoven's String Quartet in A minor (Op. 132) will be the best example of this difficulty.

TECHNIQUE 19

To the inexperienced listener who does not understand the modal scales this movement sounds as if it were written in C major and ended in F (the subdominant). To one who has thoroughly mastered the characteristics and nature of modal scales it will sound as if written in F, with the B natural proper to the mode, and ending on its correct and satisfying final. A step towards assimilating this very difficult fact may be made by playing the example given above, first with all the B's flattened, and immediately afterwards as it is written with B natural, clearly remembering that the B natural is the fourth degree of the Lydian mode and has nothing to do with the seventh (leading note to C).

Until the student of modal writing can appreciate each scale for itself, he is not a master of this part of his craft. [There can be no better study recommended in this branch of counterpoint than the Magnificats of Palestrina which are written in all the modes.] As soon as he does appreciate it, he will find that the weapons of his armoury are multiplied by three, and that he will have many additional sources of diatonic treatment to vary his conceptions before he need call upon chromatics. It will teach him to be able to stay in one key without producing a sense of monotony or lack of colour (cf. the finale of Beethoven's Fifth Symphony), and so to carry out Wagner's admirable advice to young composers to "say everything they have got to say in one key before they leave it."

It will cultivate economy of material, and so incidentally increase his command over gradations of colour. It will lay the foundations of natural and grateful writing for the human voice, upon the requirements of which the rules as to skips and combinations are entirely based. When the principles of strict counterpoint are thoroughly grasped, the writing of good harmony will become as easy as that of good counterpoint is difficult, but the difficulties of counterpoint are far more musically interesting, and the pleasure of surmounting them far greater.

So far we have dealt with the counterpoint of concurrent melodies (including double counterpoint, which is the interchange of concurrent melodies). The student must then attack the counterpoint of cross-current melodies, which go by the names of Imitation, Canon and Fugue. Of these branches of study it is unnecessary to write here, further than to insist that to be effective and useful to the composer's equipment, the work he does in them *must sound well:* that the best canons are those which are not heard unless they are looked for, and which come naturally without aggressively asserting themselves (a magnificent specimen of really musical and expressive canon is to be found in the second Agnus of Palestrina's *Missa Brevis*): that the best fugues are those which are most musically as well as logically carried to a finish, and in which the episodes, such as occur after the

TECHNIQUE 21

first entries of the subject are complete, are not inferior in interest to the corresponding passages of a sonata or a symphony. When the study of harmony (or the science of chord treatment) is tackled, it is of the highest importance to work out exercises with a contrapuntal eye, following the same principles of writing parts at once interesting in themselves, and conducing to movement and avoidance of monotony.

Cultivate ease in dealing with inversions and use roots sparingly in the bass. The perpetual insistence of root basses is one of the greatest pitfalls of the beginner; it hampers his treatment of the part, which is second only in importance to the melody, and impedes the power of free modulation, to which the study of harmony is the entrance gate. Into this domain it is unnecessary at this point for this treatise to intrude, as it has to do with the result of technical study for which ample educational literature of all degrees of merit can be found. The technical equipment of a composer, then, may be thus summed up in the order which will best benefit him.

1. The study of the pure scale.
2. Concurrent counterpoint (including modal counterpoint).
3. Harmony and modulation.
4. Cross-current counterpoint (canon, fugue, etc.).

Just, however, as no school-boy will progress without holiday or fresh air, so no budding composer can assimilate or digest all this difficult diet without amusing himself meanwhiles; and too much stress cannot be laid on the importance of encouraging him to write anything which suggests itself to him alongside his stiff studies. Such temporary freedom keeps the engines of the brain oiled, and free compositions written while technical study is progressing are valuable tests of the ability of the writer to profit by his advancing technique. If it is neglected or forbidden, spontaneity may be injured, and either the Philistine or revolutionary spirit may get the upper hand. The following short maxims may be fitly set down at this point:

1. Study counterpoint first, and through counterpoint master harmony.
2. Study strict counterpoint only.
3. Study the pure scale and accustom yourself to think in it.
4. Practise canonic and fugal writing until the results sound quite easy, natural and musical.
5. Write always some music in any free style, without thinking about rules, alongside your technical work.
6. Learn the value of using plenty of rests.

CHAPTER III

RHYTHM

IF melody is the life-blood of music, rhythm is the heart-beat or pulse which drives it. Hans von Bülow pointed out this in his trenchant way when he formulated the text (as amended by himself), "In the beginning was rhythm." There can be no life without it; if the pulse is too slow or intermittent, the sense of movement is hampered; if it is too feverish or overloaded, the music becomes fussy and restless; but the pulse must be there or vitality ceases. The study of rhythm is beyond the scope of this book, and must be prosecuted with the help of such special treatises as Hauptmann's "Harmony and Metre." For practical purposes, however, a few salient points must be touched upon here.

The first principle to grasp is the essential difference between quantity and accent. Poetry will supply the clearest examples of this distinction. A Latin hexameter line is in six feet of dactyls ($-\smile\smile$) and spondees ($--$).

$$\{-- \mid -\smile\smile \mid -- \mid -\smile\smile \mid -\smile\smile \mid --$$
$$\{-\smile\smile \mid -- \mid -\smile\smile \mid -- \mid -\smile\smile \mid --$$

The quantity of the first line of Virgil's *Aeneid* is

$$-\smile\smile \mid -\smile\smile \mid -- \mid -- \mid -\smile\smile \mid --$$
Arma virumque cano, Trojae qui primus ab oris.

The accent of the same line when read is

　　Árma virúmque cáno, Trójae qui prímus ab oris.

An example from English blank verse (five feet of iambics (⌣ —)), the first line of *Paradise Lost*, will also illustrate this point:

　　⌣ — | ⌣ — | ⌣— | ⌣ — | ⌣ — ‖
　　(*a*) Of man's first disobedience, and the fruit.

which when it is read will give the following accents:

　　(*b*) Of mán's fírst disobédience, and the frúit.

The difference between prosody and accent in this line, written out in terms of quantity alone, can be shown thus:

　　(*a*) ⌣ — ⌣ — ⌣ — ⌣ — ⌣ —
　　(*b*) ⌣ — — ⌣ ⌣ — ⌣ — ⌣ —

(*a*) is the rhythm, which drives the poetry: (*b*) is the melody, which uses the rhythm for its own purposes.

Rhythm may be roughly divided into two sections: rhythm of detail, and rhythm of phrase.

I. RHYTHM OF DETAIL.

It is obvious that the number of ways in which the notes of the scale (even including chromatic intervals) can be interchanged in order to form melodies must be limited, however numerous those ways may be. It is the entry of rhythm into the scheme which practically turns what is finite into what is infinite, and makes it possible for several composers to write an identical sequence of notes, and yet produce a wholly different effect with them; each specimen may even be stamped with the unmistakeable individuality of the writer. The following sequence of notes

appears in the finale of Beethoven's Eroica Symphony, thus:

and in the introduction to the third act of Wagner's Lohengrin, thus:

But it would be an absurdity to say that the latter was suggested by the former, or to deny to each form of the same melody the hall-mark of its inventor. The following specimens of some few of the rhythmical variations of the scale of F major will further illustrate this:

and so on *ad infinitum*.

Command over rhythm is as necessary in subsidiary parts as in the melodic. One rhythmical figure can give a character of its own to a whole movement (*e.g.* the finale of Beethoven's Seventh Symphony), and even to a whole symphony (Schumann in D minor), and will itself breed other cognate rhythms to vary it and check monotony. Its importance in song writing will be discussed when vocal music is considered. Rhythm is the first attempt of barbarians to express themselves musically, and its prime necessity as an integral part of music is proved by the fact that all the most advanced and complex works in modern music are still dependent upon it for a livelihood, as witness the *Rattenfänger* of Hugo Wolf, or the battle-section of Strauss' *Heldenleben*. All the leading motives in the *Nibelungen* are either rhythmical melody, such as the sword-theme (*alias* the common chord of C),

or rhythmical figure, such as the Nibelung-theme,

RHYTHM

(three notes of the scale of G minor). The best possible studies in rhythm are the songs of Schubert, which provide an amazing series of all sorts and kinds of figure in a short space. But let it be remembered that they are all the outcome of spontaneous invention; if they had been hunted for or manufactured, sincerity would not be so patent upon every page. Genuine rhythmical invention, like melodic, comes to the composer because it must, not because he makes it. The study of the rhythm of others must be directed rather to the way the masters use it than to the actual rhythms themselves. Manufacture will not do, but an all-round knowledge of their methods of using it will, to an inventive mind, suggest rhythms of its own creation.

II. RHYTHM OF PHRASE.

This branch of the study is of much larger scope, and has to do with the balance of general design rather than with the patterns which form the ground note of the design. It is this which enables a composer to write sentences which are intelligible and logical in their relationship to each other, and at the same time to preserve their relative proportion.

This species of rhythm exactly answers to metre in poetry. As an example of the simplest form of musical metre in four-bar and two-bar phrases, the following theme from Beethoven's *Ruins of Athens* used by him for the pianoforte variations (Op. 76) will suffice:

MUSICAL COMPOSITION

A is a four-bar sentence;
B is a four-bar sentence balancing A;
C is a two-bar sentence;
D is a two-bar sentence balancing C;
E is a four-part sentence balancing A and B.

The exact counterpart in poetical metre of this scheme is the nonsense rhyme or "Limerick," for example:

A
There was a young lady of Tyre
B
Who swept the loud chords of the lyre.
C
At the sound of each sweep
D
She enraptured the deep,
E
And enchanted the people of Tyre.

RHYTHM

(As the tune given above is Turkish, the rhyme may not be thought incongruous.)

In order to gain complete control over metrical phrasing, it is well to experiment in phrases of three, five, six, and seven bars, and to invent melodies which, although expressed in these less common sentences, yet, owing to their rhythmical proportion, completely satisfy the ear. An example of the use of a five-bar phrase as the principal section of a theme is to be found in the Russian dance (also used by Beethoven for variations):

A five bars, B five bars, C two bars, D two bars, E five bars.

        B balances A;
        D balances C;
        E balances A and B.

The two-bar rhythm at C and D gives exactly the right contrast of simplicity to the complex character of A, B and E; and for that purpose the choice of two bars, in preference to any other number, is the most satisfying. A little close investigation will show the reason. A can be subdivided into two subsections, one (α) of three and the other (β) of two bars; the two-bar portion of this in B is the basis of the melody after the double bar, and therefore the length of two bars is best adapted to this section of the melody. But, it might be urged, why not make the sections C and D one phrase of five bars exactly proportionate to A, B and E? If the phrase after the double bar were to be written as follows:

the result is to make the whole run of the tune more stiff and stodgy. The only way of securing any contrast, while preserving the five bars, would be to write the phrase in two-bar and three-bar rhythm, to balance the three-bar and two-bar rhythm of A, B and E thus:

but the ear will still wish for the relief of a simple rhythm after the two complex rhythms, and both sections will gain by their juxtaposition. For an example of this interplay of usual and unusual

RHYTHM

rhythmical phrases on a large scale, the student is referred to the famous passage in the scherzo of Beethoven's Ninth Symphony, marked "Ritmo di tre battute" and "Ritmo di quattro battute."

In addition to the juxtaposition of rhythmical phrases the composer must study the overlapping of them, the end of one period forming the beginning of the next. The following examples from Beethoven's Quartet in E flat (Op. 127) will show the working of this method:

The phrase B overlaps A by one note, and the phrase C begins on the first beat of the eighth bar, while the phrase B ends on the second beat of the same bar. The student is advised to find out examples of this for himself, and to analyse the results.

It is this aspect of rhythm which eventually enlarges and extends itself into form. Form is rhythm of phrase on a large scale, and the mind which has thoroughly assimilated the subtleties of proportion in small things will the more readily adapt itself to preserving proper balance in the design of larger conceptions. But as without contrapuntal technique it is impossible to progress in combining and enriching melodies, so without working through the initial stages of rhythm of phrase it is impossible to obtain a sure grasp of the principles of form. For the purposes of this book it will be more convenient and less hampering to the student to discuss the aspects and bearings of form after the initial stages of free composition have been entered upon, as it has to do with its larger developments; the sense of proportion which will have been gained by the study of rhythmical phrasing is sufficient, up to a certain point, in keeping the composer in the straight path of progress. As he ascends the smaller hills of invention his horizon will widen of itself, and he will gain the experience necessary to attack the snow peaks with a sense of security which will enable him to face with confidence the dangers and difficulties which lie in the path to their summits.

CHAPTER IV

MELODIES AND THEIR SIMPLE TREATMENT

THE first attempt of the tyro usually takes the form of writing a song. This is probably because the lilt of a poem suggests a musical phrase, stirs the lyrical feeling, and perhaps appeals to the dramatic sense which composers must possess in order to be composers at all. But the tyro does not know, what in course of time he will infallibly find out, that to write a good song is one of the most difficult tasks which a composer can set himself. Song writing is miniature painting. The detail must be perfect from the first note to the last, capable of being examined under the microscope, and standing the test without showing a flaw. It demands a power, which is perhaps the hardest of all to acquire, of suggesting large and comprehensive ideas in a confined and economical space, and expressing small and dainty ideas without overloading them on the one hand or underestimating them on the other.

It is also a dangerous rut in the composer's road. It seems to him smooth enough to progress in, but is likely enough to upset him when he tries to get out of it. To write a good melody or theme in absolute music by the suggestion of music itself will be doubly and trebly more difficult when the crutches of suggestive poetry are not there to lean on. The wisest plan is to keep song writing for an occasional and experimental amusement, and to eschew it as a practice until the power over writing absolute music is assured. First attempts, then, ought to be in the direction of melodic writing for an instrument, and preferably for the violin, which can play them in the pure scale. Write a melody in intelligible sentences, which is logical and clear in tonality, and to that melody *write a good bass.* Do not trouble about the intervening parts, they will come of themselves, and, to any one who knows his technique, with the minimum of trouble. The musical value of this small work will depend upon the two elements which are the product of invention, the beauty of the melody and the suggestiveness of its foundation, the bass.

When a song was brought to Brahms for criticism, he invariably covered up the right hand part of the pianoforte accompaniment before he looked at it, and primarily judged it by its melody and its bass. The rest, he said, were "trimmings." As to the best lines to take in developing a melody, no better advice can be given than Wagner, by the mouth of Hans Sachs, gives to Walther Stolzing in the *Meistersinger.*

A short summary of the scene in the third act, when Walther sings to Sachs the first version of the Preislied and Sachs' commentaries thereon, will be more illuminating than any textbook prose.[1]

---

[1] This translation is by Mr. Frederick Jameson.

MELODIES AND THEIR TREATMENT

Walther. But how by rules shall I begin?

Sachs. First make your rules, and keep them then.
Think only on your vision's beauty:
To guide you well shall be my duty.

Walther then sings the first verse, eleven bars.

Sachs. That was a "Stanza," and take good heed;
Another like it must now succeed.

Walther. Wherefore alike?

Sachs. To make it plain.
To all men, that you to wed are fain.

(Sachs' similes are drawn from the idea of a man, a wife, and the children; in other words, the idea of natural development and evolution.)

Walther sings the second verse.

Sachs. You ended in another key:
That Masters blame, you know;
But I, Hans Sachs, your meaning see;
In spring it needs must be so.

(Sachs is opposed to hard and fast rules being imported into the domain of free composition; and his principles of tuition are not those which manufacture Philistines on the one hand and revolutionaries on the other. But he approves a licence when it has a meaning and a reason in the mind of the inventor.)

Sachs. An "Aftersong" now sing as well.

(What we should term a Coda.)

Walther. What meaneth that?

Sachs. The child will tell.

(Walther has sung the "husband" stanza and the "wife" stanza.)

If true and fitly mated,
The pair by you united;
Tho' like the stanzas, yet its own,

(That is, on the same lines but independent of them.)

> And here must be both rhyme and tone.
> Let it be shapely found and neat;
> Such children parents gladly greet;
> Your stanzas so will find an end,
> And all things will together blend.

(Literally, that nothing of the previous material be thrown away.)

Walther then sings the Aftersong, or closing stanza of the first verse. Sachs says the melody is a little free, but he does not object.

When Walther in the final scene sings the Preislied again, it is most instructive to notice how he has absorbed Sachs' advice as to the second stanza and made his free modulation clearer to the ear by extending and elaborating it.

Sachs' advice may then be summed up as follows:

Know your rules but make them subservient to your poetical idea and melodic invention.

Balance your phrases so that they at once contrast with and supplement each other.

Make your chief melodic phrase clear, even by repetition, so that the ear may grasp what you are driving at.

If you make an innovation, show by the way you make it that you understand the why and wherefore of it.

Do not waste your material, and gather up your threads at the end.

Be careful to keep your tonality clear.

We will now endeavour to show the construction of a melody in absolute music, and the manner in which

MELODIES AND THEIR TREATMENT 37

it is helped by a good and suggestive bass. The best example for our purpose will be the theme from the ballet of *The Men of Prometheus*, by Beethoven, which he utilised both for pianoforte variations and for the finale (in variation form) of the Eroica Symphony. The theme is as follows:

The number of phrases is the same as in the examples from the *Ruins of Athens*. But the first four notes are the key to the tune, and their repetition a tone higher emphasises this. The first phrase (A), therefore, is a compound of two shorter phrases. This is the husband of Hans Sachs' sermon. The second phrase (B) is in one uninterrupted run; but it has a new feature of its own in the three repeated B's in the fifth bar, while it shows its relationship to A in the seventh bar (compare bars three and one). This is the wife. The next two phrases (C and D) recall the repeated B's in the second phrase, and are closely like each other, and the last phrase (E) resembles both the husband (A) in the

first four notes and the wife (B) in the last two bars.
These are the children. The whole section after the
double-bar, which is (in miniature) Sachs' Aftersong,
sums up all the material before it, so that "none of
it is lost," while it expresses related ideas in a new
way.

To this theme Beethoven has written a bass so
melodic and suggestive that he has used it apart from
the melody as a theme in itself:

So perfectly do they fit that they can be treated
with the melody below and the bass above (in double
counterpoint) as agreeably to the ear as in their
original position.

To Sachs' advice it is possible to add one clause,
which is absent from his criticism probably because
the melody he was listening to possessed the quality to
which we allude, sense of climax. All good themes
are in curves, and tend towards one striking moment
which forms the culminating point of the melody. It
need not necessarily be a climax of height: it need
only be the outstanding main feature of the whole
melody. It must come in the right place, neither too
early nor too late. In the theme given above
the climax comes at the pause and following four
notes. It is here attained by the force of the
melody itself, and not by its being a higher note than
the rest.

MELODIES AND THEIR TREATMENT 39

Another specimen of a melody, with a bass as perfect for its purpose as the theme itself, is the song "An die Musik" of Schubert. The chief characteristic of this tune is the frequent fall of a sixth, which gives the unity of idea; this is twice intensified by extending it to a seventh at (α) and to an octave with intervening notes at (β). The climax comes in the penultimate phrase which is marked ⟨.

The whole is clamped together by two falls of a sixth (emphasising the chief feature) in the final phrase:

This tune, although it bears the stamp of rapid spontaneous invention in every phrase, will bear analysis up to the hilt, and will repay it. Notice, therefore, the following points:

The balance of B to A. The phrase A falling at its close, but the phrase B rising and thus leading the interest on.

2. C and D, though two phrases (D being a variation of C), so joined that they sound like one.

3. E beginning with an intensification of D, and suggesting also an intensification of the close of A.

MELODIES AND THEIR TREATMENT 41

4. F, a summing up of the characteristic falls in A and B.

It must not be imagined for a moment from reading this cold and dry analysis that such a melody as this can be made by calculation. We cannot explain the process known as inspiration; we can, however, apply the touchstone of the best inspirations of others to test the value of our own, and we can by comparison and analysis train our minds to present the results of inspiration in their most perfect form. A melody is not necessarily in its most perfect state when it is first written down. Some of the finest tunes in the world have gone through long processes of lengthening, shortening, refining and altering in various ways before they have reached the form in which the world now knows them. The first stages of the immortal theme of Beethoven's Ninth Symphony are almost absurd to look back upon, *e.g.*:

All the other countless modifications and transformations which this theme went through before it emerged from the chrysalis are to be found in the sketch books of Beethoven (edited by Nottebohm),[1] a collection which ought to be on the study table of every composer.

Fortunately for the student, Beethoven wrote down all the processes of his thoughts and the working out of them on paper, and, still more fortunately, they have been to a great extent preserved. The sketch books are of a value as inestimable to a composer as Albert Dürer's sketches are to a painter. They give the same clue to his method of working as the unfinished corner of Rembrandt's portrait of Burgomaster Six gives to that artist's technique. It is not necessary to be a German scholar to follow the main points of this unique collection or the direction of Beethoven's studies, although a fair knowledge of the language will enable the student to get many an illuminating hint from Nottebohm's comments. Two examples of the way in which Beethoven worked upon and improved his melodies may be given. They are from the first and last movements of the well-known Sonata in F major (Op. 24) for pianoforte and violin.

[1] *Beethoveniana* and *Zweite Beethoveniana,* von Gustav Nottebohm. Leipzig: J. Reiter-Biedermann. 1887.

MELODIES AND THEIR TREATMENT

Note how the end of the melody is revived so as to recall the opening by the development of α and β; also that Beethoven founds his theme on the diatonic scale, and treats chromatic intervals only as additional colour, of which more anon.

It is clear from these specimens that the initial idea of both themes is the groundwork of what may be termed the inspiration, and that without altering that feature he has worked upon every subsequent bar, polishing and improving at every step. The plan, however, both of modulation and of rhythmical balance remains as it first occurred to him. Many instances will be found in these books of themes which would make the reputation of any composer as they stood, but which Beethoven considered crude and unfinished, and are only shown to be so by the wonderful results of his refining fires. Perhaps the most amazing example of this careful weighing and striving after perfection is to be found on page 55 *et seq.* of *Beethoveniana I.*, where the last four-bar phrase of the variation movement in the String Quartet, Op. 131 (C sharp minor) is modified no less than fifteen times, and appears in the printed copy in a sixteenth shape! To a less scrupulous composer, almost any of the first fifteen versions would have sufficed.

There remains the question as to the diatonic or chromatic treatment of melodies. We possess in western music no interval less than a semitone (except in the form of *portamento*). Chromatics are, as their name implies, colour and not drawing. If we use in excess the only means we have of heightening effect, we have nothing further to fall back upon for intensifying contrast.

MELODIES AND THEIR TREATMENT 45

Mozart, who was a past master of chromatic writing, never went a step too far in the use of them; as, for instance, the Andante of his Third Quartet in E flat, where he anticipates the first phrase of Wagner's *Tristan und Isolde* and rounds it off with masterly diatonic contrast.

Tristan itself, which teems with chromatics, becomes immediately diatonic at its moments of climax, such as the coming of the ship in the third act (where the scale and chord of C pounds away with the insistence of Beethoven himself), and wherever the healthy, muscular, kindly figure of Kurwenal comes to the front. Practically all the bigger and most important motives of the *Nibelungen* are also diatonic, such as the Walhalla theme and the sword theme. Of the *Meistersinger* it is unnecessary to speak, diatonics are written large upon every page of it. Wagner himself in his earlier and less masterly days occasionally weakened a melody by making it rely upon a chromatic progression. The phrase in the Tannhäuser March, and still more the first phrase of the "Song to the Evening Star," are instances of this.

When he uses a similar progression in the Preislied, it produces a totally different impression,

precisely because in the former instances the chromatics are essential, and in the second (as in the Beethoven example given above) they are ornamental. In the latter he was the master of chromatics; in the former he was their servant. It is better to learn from Wagner the assured master, than from Wagner the budding innovator and experimenter.

Historical investigation will perhaps rightly ascribe this early tendency of Wagner to rely too freely on chromatic progressions to the influence (surprisingly far-reaching in the early part of the nineteenth century) of Spohr. It will hardly be believed that about 1840 Spohr was looked upon by many modernists of the day as the superior of Beethoven, an opinion which even survived to a period within the recollection of the present writer. Spohr was hailed as the progressist, and Beethoven was written down as (to use the jargon of the present day) the academic, while Bach was invariably described as a dry-as-dust calculator. The fact is that Spohr has to thank his chromatics both for his meteoric rise and his rapid fall. They tickled the palate vastly, but in the end wholesome food prevailed as a diet over pickles and jam. But Wagner owed much to Spohr, who, for all his musical fads and shortcomings, was a broad-minded, far-seeing critic, and who, by the production of *The Flying Dutchman*, held out the first hand to its young author. That Wagner was influenced at first by Spohr's most striking mannerism is not to be wondered at, though he was too great a man to be hidebound by it for long, and he soon found out the proper proportion of condiments to use with his diet. That he always retained a soft spot in his heart for Spohr was evident from his travelling a long distance in 1874 to hear the revival of *Jessonda*, at which the writer was present. History repeats itself sometimes in the transient exaltation of the compounders of nerve-stimulants over the purveyors of sound food. We let ourselves be beguiled by the beauty of the jars of coloured water in the chemist's window, and turn away from the dry, academic and unaesthetic aspect of the baker's shop.

The advice, therefore, to the student under this heading may thus be summed up:

Trust to inspiration for a melody.

Do not necessarily be satisfied with the form in which it first presents itself, but work at the details while preserving its balance.

When your melody satisfies you, get a bass for it which is as melodious as you can make it without allowing it to overshadow the melody proper. The bass will probably be in your mind as you write the melody.

Practise as much as possible in old rhythmical dance-forms, such as minuets, sarabands, allemandes. Vary the number of bars in your phrases, and be careful to balance them satisfactorily to the ear. Remember that sentences to be intelligible must have commas, semicolons, colons, and full stops, and apply this principle to your music. By doing so you will make your phrases as clear to the listener as they are, even in their cruder form, to yourself.

Found your melodies on the diatonic scale, and treat chromatics as reinforcements and decorations only, until your themes move easily in diatonic intervals.

CHAPTER V

THE COMPLEX TREATMENT OF MELODIES. VARIATIONS

THE next step is to combine rhythm of detail with rhythm of phrase, and to use both for the purpose of varying the treatment of melodies. The simplest way of varying the treatment of a melody is to alter the harmonies which underlie it, as in the following phrase from "God save the King":

which can be varied in harmony thus:

This kind of variation is mere child's play to any one who knows his harmony, but for the purposes of composition it is only useful as a framework to be filled in by rhythmical phrases, and as indicating a scheme of modulation. The simple treatment of a melody has to do with its bass only, and with the working out of the materials of those two parts. The complex treatment involves using intermediate parts which will complete the harmonic scheme and add interest to its presentment. The first may be said to be the building standing on secure foundations, complete in its architectural proportions, but empty and bare. The second is the painting and furnishing of the empty building. The decorations must be in keeping with the style of the architecture, and sufficiently varied to give due contrast without disturbing the general design.

This treatment of melodies must be practised both for voices and instruments. The most useful method is to begin with voices. Choose a hymn tune or a chorale, and, after harmonising it freely in four or five parts, take the melody as a Canto Fermo in long notes in one part and write three or four free parts round it. Brahms' motet, "A Saving Health," is a compact and admirable model of this style of treatment; the phrases of the chorale are treated in intelligible sections or sentences, and the free parts are all founded upon the phrases which they accompany. For the harmonisation of the tune itself innumerable prototypes can be found in Bach, many of them modern and experimental enough to satisfy, and even to surprise, the most ultra-progressive taste. The same groundwork will do equally well for instrumental treatment, and here again a close study of

MELODIES AND VARIATIONS

Bach's Organ Chorales will supply the best lesson as to complex methods of accompanying a melody, some of them, in addition, showing how the chorale tune itself can be modified and varied to suit the general character of the piece. Brahms' Chorale Preludes for Organ are also most valuable examples for study. It is unnecessary to specify any, when all this vast treasure-house is within the reach of every student. He must not, however, be content with playing them through, but must study closely the texture of the individual parts and the ways in which they interweave and combine. This branch of composition leads naturally, and, indeed, dovetails into, the writing of variations.

Variations are to free composition what counterpoint is to technique — the master-key of the whole building. Interesting in themselves to elaborate, they are of still greater service in training the mind to deal easily with the most difficult problems in works of larger proportions. Sections of sonata form, such as the episodes between the statements of themes, the development (or free fantasia), and the coda, all depend upon the knowledge of writing variations; and the repetitions of the main themes themselves become far more intrinsically interesting in the hands of a composer who is well practised in variation writing. It should be clearly understood that we do not use the term variation from the point of view of mere ornamentation or passage writing on the basis of a theme. It is easy even among the old masters to distinguish those who knew every nook and corner of this branch of their craft from those who did not, by comparing their powers in this form.

The greatest masters of it were, without question, Bach, Beethoven and Brahms. To them variations meant the extraction of the essence of the theme, a freedom of development which amounted to new inventions founded upon old ideas, an extraordinary power of twining, twisting and juggling with the details of themes, of presenting them in lights illuminated by their own individuality, and of exemplifying what has been touched upon in the chapter on rhythm, the ability to turn the conceptions of others into an original conception of their own.

In this connection we may specify three of the most masterly examples from the works of these composers — the Goldberg Variations of Bach, the Diabelli Variations of Beethoven, and the Haydn Variations of Brahms; after these, *non longo intervallo*, the Études Symphoniques of Schumann and the Symphonic Variations of Dvořák. When we compare these with the "Harmonious Blacksmith" and the well-known "Passacaglia" in the Piano Suite of Handel, or with the Pianoforte Variations of Schubert, the difference becomes patent at once. Handel, for all his massive power, did not attempt more than the repetition of the whole theme over and over again, with a series of embroidered passages. Schubert, who himself admitted his lack of technical training, and regretted it so deeply that he began to study hard only in the last years of his life, seldom advanced further than Handel's type of variation. The others, whose technical armour was complete, fought with perfected weapons, attacked difficulties which would have been insurmountable without them, and came out easy victors.

It will be as well to follow out the path which they

MELODIES AND VARIATIONS

took, and to explore for ourselves the country they discovered and mapped out. It is unnecessary to print at length the examples of variations which will be analysed here. All that the student requires for the purpose of following the illustrations are a copy of Beethoven's pianoforte works, and of Brahms' Variations on the Chorale St. Antoni of Haydn.

I. THE THEME.

Whether the composer writes or chooses his theme he must bear in mind three essentials: firstly, that it should contain sufficient material to vary; secondly, that it should have at least one striking feature; thirdly, that it should be simple. Abundance of suggestive material is a self-evident necessity. If there is not enough contrast in the phrases, the writer will run dry of ideas for the variations. But they should only be suggestions, which the variations may be left to elaborate. In the theme of the Prometheus Variations given in the former chapter there are at least five such phrases. The first two bars, the repeated notes in the fifth bar, the figure 𝅘𝅥𝅮𝅘𝅥𝅮𝅘𝅥 𝅘𝅥𝅮𝅘𝅥𝅮𝅘𝅥 in the seventh bar, the scale followed by the three repeated quavers in the ninth and tenth bars, and the whole of the bass, which itself contains other suggestive phrases.

Then as to the striking feature. This may be attained in many ways, either by an unusual melodic progression or modulation, or by a modification of tempo (such as the pause in the same example), or by a strong dynamic contrast, or by an unusual rhythm in the phrases of the melody itself. The first three explain themselves, and examples are innumerable.

Of the fourth it is as well to give two typical examples — the Chorale St. Antoni of Haydn and the theme of Schumann used by Brahms for his Four-hand Variations (Op. 23). In the former of these the scheme of rhythm is 5, 5, || 4, 4, 4, 4, 3. The last two four-bar rhythms in the second part are really two five-bar rhythms with the first bar of each succeeding rhythm overlapping the last bar of the previous one.

Similarly, the first bar of the final three bars overlaps the previous rhythm.

In the theme of Schumann the scheme is 4, 4, 4, 4, || 4, 4, 4, ||, the second part being less by one four-bar rhythm than the first. The theme in A major (the Russian Dance) used by Beethoven for variations, and quoted at length in the second chapter of this book, may be also referred to. Here the scheme runs, 5, 5, || 4, 5.
(2+2)

The striking features in the Haydn theme are twofold, viz. the rhythm of the phrases and the nine times repeated B flats at the end.

(Compare the three B flats in the Beethoven Prometheus theme.)

MELODIES AND VARIATIONS

This is only another aspect of Hans Sachs' advice to trust to repetition in order to grip the attention. As some peculiar feature in the face of an ancestor will often reappear in his descendants, even when in other respects they are unlike, so in variations the family likeness will be preserved in the children of the theme, if it possesses some such distinguishing characteristic; and no matter how far their physiognomy apparently diverges from their point of origin, they will always "throw back" enough to establish their identity as part of the family if this feature is preserved.

Thirdly, a theme should be expressed in as simple terms as possible, at any rate for purposes of practice. An over-elaborated theme is at once a variation and robs a composer of one of his series. The tendency in a beginner is always to write a variation for a theme, and an admirable corrective is to extract from this variation its simplest form of expression — in arithmetical language, to find its least common multiple. Great care must be exercised to avoid, on the one hand, the excision of any of the important features, or, on the other, the retention of any that are unnecessary.

In addition to the kind of theme mentioned above, there is another most useful type, which, however, as it is more difficult to handle, had best be practised after the theme in rhythmical phrases has been mastered. This type is the short form of which Bach's Chaconne for the Violin and Passacaglia for the Organ, Beethoven's thirty-two Variations for Pianoforte in C minor, and the Finale of Brahms' Fourth Symphony in E minor are the best possible examples. In order to tackle variation writing on this species of theme, the student must have the treatment of ground basses (which is an important part of his harmony technique) at his fingers' ends. A simple example of it, showing how much can be accomplished with limited means, and yet with the maximum of musical interest, is Dido's Lament from Purcell's *Dido and Aeneas*.[1]

II. THE VARIATIONS.

The methods of writing variations are so numerous as to be practically illimitable. The simplest way to begin is by variation of movement, starting with slow gradation and increasing the speed of the note-values; *e.g.* if the phrase

were to be varied, the following would be a few of the gradations of this type:

---

[1] It is scarcely too much to say that Purcell was the greatest master of variation writing before the time of Bach; witness his sonata in variation form for two violins, bass and harpsichord, on a ground bass.

MELODIES AND VARIATIONS 57

From this we can proceed to rhythmical changes.

When to this wide field are added the varyings of pace, of modulation, of changes of key (major and minor), of seriousness and of humour, and of ranges of force, the composer will appreciate the enormous store of materials upon which he can draw.

We will now analyse a most interesting set of variations on a most uninteresting theme, the twenty-four Pianoforte Variations on the Arietta "Vieni amore" of Righini, by Beethoven. So silly is the air which he has set himself to vary that we are almost tempted to consider the work as a specimen of what his waggish nature could do with the most unpromising materials he could find. (Compare the waltz for which the publisher Diabelli tormented him and every other Viennese composer to write variations.) Childish, however, as the theme is, it has three contrasts of phrase, thus:

There we must note (*a*) the staccato notes in I.; (*b*) the slurs in II.; (*c*) the skips, and the group of semiquavers in III.; (*d*) the general "lie" of the theme, such as the descending scale in the first half, which in itself forms no small part of the variation scheme. How does Beethoven develop this "Three Blind Mice" material?

(The student must now compare the following analysis with the pianoforte copy.)

Var. 1. The theme itself varied and ornamented, the harmony enriched, a most interesting bass added to II., and the end of II. made melodically beautiful. III. rhythmically altered as well as melodically, the semiquaver movement being transferred to the middle of the second part. The close altered to an ending on the fifth, which carries on the feeling of expectation.

Var. 2. A persistent figure throughout in sharp

short rhythm; the C flattened in bar two, the modulation and the melody both altered; the accompanying chords being transferred to the second and fourth quavers of the bar (the off beats). Alternate *p* and *f* (dynamic variation).

Var. 3. The slurs of II. inserted into I., and the melody given in quavers to admit of it. A scale from the bass running across the melody in both parts, and the melody crossing into the bass.

Var. 4. The same idea as the treatment of the scale in variation applied in the form of shakes. The melody transferred to the bass and much altered, the slurs of the last variation extended from two bars to four, and the section II. still more drastically altered.

Var. 5. A brilliant and ornamental variation, the figure being in the treble, and the theme (a third higher) in the bass. A suggestion for the first time of change of key; the earlier portion of III. being in the tonic minor, and so making the major ending much more fresh in quality.

Var. 6. The slurs of the third variation applied throughout; the scheme is orchestral, suggesting clarinets and bassoons; the whole is (with the exception of the closing chord) in two parts only, doubled. The repeat of the second part is written out in full to allow of a variation of it, the lower parts being transferred to the upper, and *vice versa*. Chromatics enter now into the scheme.

Var. 7. Contrapuntal and polyphonic in style, the second note converted into a rhythmical figure, which persists throughout. The idea of the crossing scale in the third variation applied in III. to the new figure. Many more marks of expression.

Var. 8. Semiquaver movement prevails, the last four bars of II. strongly insisting on the semiquaver figure suggested by the theme.

Var. 9. Four sections of a phrase in chromatic thirds, followed by two strong chords, but reversed each time in succession, thus recalling the general lie of the theme. Pianistically laid out.

Var. 10. Slurs treated so as to produce pedals (top and bottom) on tonic and dominant. The skips in III. extended and varied.

Var. 11. March rhythm introduced; monotony entirely avoided by the transference of each answering phrase to a higher position.

Var. 12. Very chromatic and in the tonic minor. A new melody invented and superimposed on an accompaniment which is itself a variation of the theme. Here again the repeat of the second part is written out in full, and the part repeated is itself altered, mainly as regards the position of the bass.

Var. 13. Another brilliant pianistic variation, closely related to the theme. Note the last variation at the end of the Ninth Symphony peeping in, as it so frequently does in the composer's works of this period.

Var. 14. Each four-bar section is repeated. Two *tempi* are employed, each section being alternately Allegretto and Adagio, and the Adagio always most fully ornamented, sometimes in the manner of a cadenza. The melody after the first four bars greatly altered, and with a moving staccato bass of a typically Beethovenish pattern.

Var. 15. Mainly ornamental. The skips of III. imported into I. and transferred to the treble, over a

MELODIES AND VARIATIONS

persistent figure of semiquaver triplets, which contain in themselves the kernel of the theme. The idea of the crossing scale reproduced at the close.

Var. 16. Cross rhythms in a semiquaver figure, and syncopations in the bass (suggested by the off-beat bass of the second variation). The two sections of each part are themselves varied by a figure with a triplet and a quaver 𝅘𝅥𝅮𝅘𝅥𝅮𝅘𝅥 which increases the brilliancy.

Var. 17. A very richly harmonised version of the theme, unaltered in the first part, and only slightly modified in the second, but with a stroke of genius at the end, where an unexpected pause is followed by a most tranquil close. (Compare the opening of Schumann's "Abendlied.") The whole is solemn, serious and dignified, and mostly on a pedal bass.

Var. 18. The ¾ time begins to lean to ⅜. The theme crosses from treble to bass every two bars. Playful in character.

Var. 19. Canonic and in two parts, altogether in ⅜ time. Notice the variety given to the second part by breaking up the figure of six quavers, assigned to each hand alternately in the first part, into contrasted groups of three.

Var. 20. Highly humorous, a joke from beginning to end. Founded on the skips of III. with a little chromatic scale intervening. No two phrases in the same position.

Var. 21. A mixture of the styles of Vars. 17 and 7. Variety gained by an unexpected start in the relative minor, which later turns out not to be the key of the variation. The second part polyphonic and canonic.

Var. 22. Related to 16. A similar cross rhythm in the semiquavers, but the theme here is in the treble and the figure in the bass.

Var. 23. *Adagio sostenuto.* Here, for the first time, Beethoven produces the effect of developing the length of the theme. An effect which he produces partly by the pace, partly by the character of a sonata slow movement which he imparts to it, and partly by repeating both halves with greatly varied treatment and a profusion of contrasted figures and ornaments. He turns the second part into a sort of duet by crossing the hands; this is an example of a variation within a variation.

Var. 24. The Finale. After a very simple variation in two parts he writes an extended coda, full of whimsical humour, in which he seems to hold the various little quips of the theme and his own previous treatment of them up to ridicule. Notice the absurd *pianissimo* D before the *Un poco meno Allegro*; the twisting of the theme into the key of B flat and back again; the excursion into the remote key of A flat, with the opening phrase interrupting itself; the gradual development of the little figure

into an *Allegro* entirely founded upon it; the return of the theme compressed into eight bars at the *Presto assai*; the semiquaver figure gradually getting slower and slower all alone as the opening bars of the theme die away in the bass, semiquavers halved to quavers, quavers to crotchets, crotchets to minims, minims to

MELODIES AND VARIATIONS 63

semibreves, and finally two humorously laid out chords of D major, into which even at the last moment he puts a cross rhythm.

The only variant upon which he has not embarked in the course of this wonderful *jeu d'esprit*, is the enlarging in actual length of the phrases of the theme; although in the twenty-third he produces the effect of doing so by an extreme modification of the pace.

The student can apply for himself the same principles of analysis to the thirty-three variations on the waltz of Diabelli (Op. 121), a theme of almost greater inanity than Righini's, but treated in a way that almost deifies the tune. The variations go so far afield that it is often necessary to compare them separately with the theme in order to be able to work out their genesis. The following variations will best illustrate this: Vars. 3, 9, 13, 14, 18, 20 (a most amazing piece of modernity), 23, 24, 28 (the ancestor of some of Schumann's children), 30, 31, 32 and 33. This work, with the variations in the C sharp minor String-Quartet (Op. 131), and the finale of the last Pianoforte Sonata (Op. 111), almost (but, as time has proved, not quite) says the last word in the modern development of this fascinating form of composition.

We will now apply the same analytical process to the Haydn Variations of Brahms, which being written originally for two pianofortes and afterwards for orchestra are naturally more complicated in structure.

The rhythmical scheme of the theme has been given above; but the detail of the first bar

must be kept closely in mind.

Var. 1. A combination of 2/4 and 6/8 time. Following his usual plan, Brahms begins at once by using one phrase of the theme as a basis of the whole variation. That phrase is the last five of the repeated B's, where their note-values are ♩ ♩ ♩ ♩ ♩.. These form a tonic pedal in the first part and a dominant pedal after the double bar, returning to the tonic after the repetition; and the original nine become eleven (by diminution) at the close. The 6/8 and 2/4 figures are heard together and, though apparently freed from the shackles of the theme, exactly preserve its chord sequence; moreover they are in double counterpoint (reversible) in the two five-bar phrases. After the double bar the same form is preserved for four bars only, and is broken up for contrast in the next four: the repetition brings a reinforced return of the opening, and in the last seven bars the opening figure of the 6/8

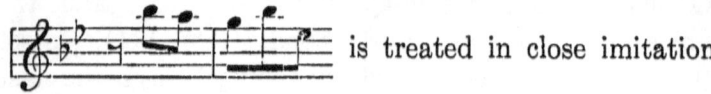 is treated in close imitation

by itself.

Var. 2. (*Più vivace*, in the tonic minor.) The phrase upon which this is built is the first three notes only of the theme, thus , and of this fragment the first two notes only are worked in Part I.

The intervening four-bar passage is itself a variation on Var. 1. The first bar of it

MELODIES AND VARIATIONS 65

is used as a figure in the second part in various guises, and finally provides the material for the close.

Var. 3. (*Con moto.*) A very tranquil and smoothly-running version, with the ♩♪ eliminated altogether. The theme is varied into a melody so individual that it is only by reading the original tune alongside the variant that its closeness to it can be appreciated. Notice the beauty of the bass, and the augmentation of ♩♫ into ♩.♪|♩ in the fourth bar (horn part). Each part of this variation is written out in full, and the repeated portion is itself varied, a semiquaver figure being added to the original scheme: this figure develops into an important running melody, first given to the oboe, and at the close distributed amongst the strings. The repeated notes appear at intervals, and at the end are syncopated.

Var. 4. (*Andante con moto* ⅜, tonic minor.) A similar double variation treatment is to be found here, and the scheme is on reversible lines like Var. 1. It is mainly laid out in three parts, and all these are interchangeable; the melody is elaborated at the repetition. The close is an insistence on the repeated B's.

Var. 5. (*Vivace.*) Of the nature of a scherzo. Also a double variation. The key figure is the first four notes of the theme upside down

¾ begins to cross ⅞. In the second part the key figure

is treated in close imitation, and the repeated B's, varied by combination with it, appear as early as the fifth bar of the second part; they are also suggested in

diminution throughout

Var. 6. (*Vivace* ¾.) The key figure is the first bar of the theme reversed, diminished into semiquavers,

and repeated twice . The

modulation at the close of the first and second five-bar phrases is to D major instead of to F major. The remainder of the opening figure is from the fourth

bar of the theme . An arpeggio

figure  to which can be traced

the germ of the melody in the succeeding variation, is frequently used in the second part.

Var. 7. (*Grazioso* ⁶⁄₈.) A very free variation, preserving all the modulations and (like all the rest) the shape of the theme. The melody, however, is new, suggesting only in bars 2 and 3 the repeated B's, and founded on the arpeggio figure in Var. 6. The rhythm of its opening preserves that of the opening of the theme. In the second part the crossing of ¾ with ⁶⁄₈, first hinted at in Var. 5, is much more

MELODIES AND VARIATIONS 67

elaborated. The repeated B's become a tonic pedal rhythm at the close, and are finally modified thus:

Var. 8. (*Presto non troppo* ¾, tonic minor.) A double variation, very contrapuntal and complicated in detail. It begins with the first three notes of the theme reversed, and in all other respects, except shape, is very independent. The theme appears in the tenth bar in the bass, and clamps the whole together. The ingenuity of the interchange and combinations of the running figures, especially in Part II., will repay the closest study.

The Finale (*Andante* ₵) is a series of variations constructed on a ground bass repeated no less than seventeen times. It is a fine example of the species of variation mentioned on p. 55 of the type of Bach's Passacaglia. The ground bass is a modification of the first bars of the theme and is itself in five-bar rhythm,

thus preserving throughout its relationship to it. The series of five-bar variations are at first so interwoven as to form a connected passage in close imitation over the first three repetitions of the bass; at the fourth repetition they begin to clear up, separate and become rhythmical again; they may be classed as follows:

    { 1.
      2. Fugue and imitation.
      3.
       4. Rhythms of 6 against 4.

5. Chord pulses.
6. Chord pulses with an added figure of quavers

7. The bass diminished and syncopated as a counterpoint above the ground, and treated also in imitation.
8. A suggestion of the tonic minor, otherwise a variant of 7.
9. Triplet quavers add to the movement, and the spirit of Var. 7 is reproduced both by the arpeggio figure and the character of the melody.
10. A syncopated modification of 9.
11. Another modification of 9 and 10, the syncopations becoming a rhythm of long crotchet triplets.
12. The long crotchet triplets become a melody in which chromatic intervals are largely used.
13. This melody is further developed and enriched with a second part; the triplet arpeggios are modified to four-quaver arpeggios.

A combined and continuous passage.
{
14. The ground bass is moved up to the treble, and the key is changed altogether to the tonic minor. The leap of a fourth at the beginning is filled up with the intervening notes, and is treated in imitation: the bass begins to modulate into the succeeding variation.
15. The quaver figure is further developed, the ground placed still higher.
}

16. The original first bar of the chorale appears in the bass, and is closely imitated elsewhere. The original theme begins to make itself felt.
17. The ground returns to the bass, the whole chorale theme, still slightly modified, gradually emerges above it.

MELODIES AND VARIATIONS

Then begins the coda. The first bar of the theme is repeated three times followed by the rest in its simple form, with a brilliant surrounding of scale passages, the last repeated B's being expanded till they sound like a written out pause, with the help of a gradual *ritardando*. The whole work concludes with a five-bar rhythm, suggesting (naturally) the repeated B's again. It is interesting to note the dynamic gradations of this series.

```
                    f   piu f            p   piu p  pp
p
1.   2.   3.   4.   5.   6.   7.   8.   9.   10.  11.   12.

              p    f           p    ff
              13.  14.  15.  16.  17.  Coda.
```

The practice of variation writing tells especially in the pianoforte part of songs (commonly called the accompaniment). A few examples may be quoted to show its bearing on this branch of composition. The last movement of Beethoven's Busslied (Op. 48, No. 6), Adelaide (Op. 46), and Der Wachtelschlag, and countless songs of Schumann are examples of this. In Schubert, who relies mainly on figure repetition, it comes rarely to the front. In Brahms more frequently than in any other song-writer. The most instructive instance to be found is in his song "An ein Bild," "To a picture" (Op. 63, No. 3, published by Peters). It is a perfect specimen of the subordination of detail to the beauty of melody, and though the ingenuity of the pianoforte part is astounding, no casual hearer would notice that there was any complicated writing at all unless his attention were directed to it. The idea of "the picture" pervades the whole song persistently, and is suggested by all sorts of variations of the opening vocal phrase, which are apparently independent of the voice part and perfect in themselves, while the melody runs along without undergoing a single modification to fit the permutations and combinations in the pianoforte part. The result is that the listener feels the influence of the picture subtly pervading the whole song without his knowing why. The melody of the first verse of the voice part is as follows:

The first five notes are the "picture" theme, thus expressed in the piano part:

and every bar of the melody is accompanied by it in various forms: (1) as above; (2) augmented; (3) diminished and twice repeated; (4) the first three notes diminished and repeated, the last two augmented and in syncopation with a new subject

MELODIES AND VARIATIONS

in the bass; (5) is the same as (4) reversed in double counterpoint. These variations are now shown in combination with the melody:

In the third and fourth verses, third line, the motive becomes a figure developed in the bass with altered intervals. The return of the first theme is introduced by two bars of pianoforte, (a) with the motive reversed and (b) in its original position, treated in imitation:

the last verse repeating the first. A first-rate musician might accompany this song at first sight without noticing all these ingenuities until his attention was called to them, so perfect a specimen is it of the *ars celare artem*.

The art of art-concealing is one of the composer's prime necessities; it is not so much a virtue to possess it, as it is a vice to lack it. The slave in Horace's satires, who asked a reward from his master because he had not stolen any of his property, was told very justly that his reward was security from the gallows. So it is with the composer. If he is not sufficiently at home and at ease in the technique of his art, any attempt to work on the lines of these variations, and even of this small song, will show effort, the machinery will creak, beauty will vanish, and the result will be a very obvious and irritating exhibition of ingenious puzzles. The master will, more often than not, write the ingenuities without knowing that he has written them, and will often be himself surprised at an analytical exposition of the interesting points of detail which his well-equipped and disciplined brain spontaneously worked out for him. This is the only art which will live and

MELODIES AND VARIATIONS

tell upon generations of men, and without it music is a barren wilderness. It is only attainable by men of inventive power, who have worked steadily, without faltering or taking their hand from the plough, to bring their workmanship to the greatest perfection possible. When an artist, who has made a design for mosaic, proceeds to put his picture together, he must make his tesserae so even-edged as to fit easily to each other; if the edges are rough and unfinished, he will not improve the effect of his design by hammering them together and chipping them; nor can he excuse such methods by pleading that the mosaic picture is so far off that no one will see the flaws. The flaws will let in the dust and damp, and the laziness of the inferior workmanship will be exposed by the great enemy of all charlatans, Time.

CHAPTER VI

FORM

It is not within the purview of this book to treat Form in all its aspects. There are treatises enough and to spare on this branch of study, which will give the student ample information as to its historical development and various guises. We have mainly to do with its use as a factor in composition. So far we have discussed what may be termed the flesh and blood of music, melodic invention and rhythmical treatment. Form may be, in similar parallel, termed the skeleton; the bones, which by their solidity prevent the flesh from being flabby and uncontrollable, and by their symmetry of position and due proportion of size, regulate the position of the flesh which covers them, producing a good or a bad figure according as their proportions are good or bad. To continue the simile, the clothes are represented by tone-colour, an adjunct without which the skeleton and the flesh and blood can live, though they cannot exist without each other. This chapter has to do with the essentials of music's life, and colour will be considered in its proper place, after the consideration of the more vital necessities.

Form has been defined by Sir Hubert Parry as the

FORM 75

means by which unity and proportion are arrived at by the relative distribution of keys and harmonic bases on the one hand, and of subjects or figures or melodies on the other. We might also describe it in the same terms as a painter would employ. The form is the composition upon his canvas, the melodies and phrases are the figures or the objects in his landscape. If he designs his picture so that he cannot get the subjects of his design into the canvas as it stands, it will not serve his purpose to add on excrescences to the edges; its shape, whether circular or square or elliptical, has to be symmetrical in order to satisfy the eye. Neither can he paint his figures, as Wiertz did, climbing out of the picture round the frame, without laying himself open to the charge of eccentricity. The word "eccentric" is the clue to the rule. Your picture must work to a centre, and you must not get outside the attraction of the centre. You must decide on the size of your canvas, and so design your subjects as to bring them within its limits, without giving the impression of its being too large or too small for them. The proportionate treatment of the subjects must conform at once to the size of the picture and to themselves, and there must be a central point to which the manner of the design irresistibly directs the eye (such as the child's head in the Sistine Madonna of Raphael). As in painting, so in music. No art is formless or it is monstrous, just as no face or figure is distorted without being repulsive. It is a law of nature against whose pricks no artist, whether he be painter, sculptor, architect, poet or musician, can kick without damage to his reputation. At the same time music has one advantage over other arts, in that, being itself a subtle and intangible entity, it can create its own forms and vary them more completely than they can. But one rule is common to them all; no matter how free the design, the proportions must be preserved if the work is to make any sensible appeal to human intelligence. A new form in music may require study and frequent hearing to understand it, but if it is logical and founded on a thorough knowledge and control of means, time will endorse it. Such modifications grow (like folk-songs in Hungary) and are not made. To have any value at all they must in their nature be children of their fathers. The laws of evolution apply as rigidly to musical art as they do to nature itself. It is not necessary to go out of the way to seek for novelty of design any more than for novelty of expression. No two faces are exactly alike, although the ears, eyes, nose and mouth are in the same relative position. To paint a face with two noses or four ears would not suggest novelty of form, but only the imbecility of the artist. Polyphemus, with his one eye in the centre of his forehead, will always be a grotesque monstrosity. In the treatment of form, as in the control of invention, the only path to originality is through sincerity of expression on the lines of natural beauty. The moment originality is forced, extravagance, exaggeration and *bizarrerie* become inevitable.

The history of musical form, then, is a history of evolution, and in order to master it, the student must evolve it for himself in miniature on the same lines that it has been evolved through the last three centuries: beginning with short dance forms, and gradually expanding his ideas into longer movements,

FORM

until he can deal with symphonies and large choral works. There are plenty of dance forms at his disposal to vary his rhythmical powers, a point of which he must never lose sight.

Minuets and all sorts of old measures can be practised first on the shortest lines, such as $\|\ 4, 4: \|$ $\|: 8, 4, 4: \|$, and later with extended phrases. The trios will give opportunity for inventing themes in contrast with, and yet suitable to, the minuets, the first step towards thoroughly contrasting first and second subjects in sonata form without destroying the family connection between them; and it will be found most valuable always to write a short coda for the conclusion, and endeavour to combine in it the ideas of the minuet and of the trio, so clamping together the whole as a small work of art.

This is exactly on the lines of Hans Sachs' advice for a master-song. The minuet is the husband, the trio is the wife, the coda is the child. From the minuet the composer may progress to its descendant the scherzo, where he had better follow the type indicated by Beethoven, not that of Mendelssohn, which is of a wholly different pattern more allied to the rondo. The scherzo will, in addition to giving plenty of opportunity for expansion, provide opportunities for practice in the writing of rapid notes, which always presents great difficulty to the beginner, and especially to one who has begun his studies with harmony instead of counterpoint. The best models for minuets will be found in Haydn and in Mozart, and for scherzos in Beethoven, Schubert and Dvořák.

Next in order of difficulty comes the rondo, the

musical equivalent of the rondeau in poetry, with its threefold repetition of the main theme. Here he will have to add a third contrasted subject, and will also be able to practise the experience he has derived from variation writing by modifying in different ways the three repetitions of the first subject as they reappear; while the episodes or bridges between the subjects will give him his first practice in the development of fragments of his themes and in the mixing of them. From rondos he may pass to slow movements both in song, rondo and elementary first-movement form, and from slow movements to sonata form proper as in the first movements of sonatas. When he has mastered this last and most difficult type, his work, as far as form is concerned, is done; but the mastery is not gained in one or even two successful attempts. The variety within the limits of an apparently shackled formula is so great, that it takes not months but years to turn form from a master into a servant. If the composer investigates the knots of the ropes which bind him, he will eventually find how to loosen them.

Too many students are afraid, from a natural desire to be original, to copy the examples which the great composers provide; but if they wish to get at the root of the methods in which their predecessors successfully worked, they must make up their minds to do so. Here, again, the parallel of the art of painting comes in, where students can get the best possible tuition from masters greater than any living by copying their pictures, and so getting at the root of their methods. A musician has one great advantage over a painter in this branch of study; for he can take a movement by a great composer for a model, but confine his imitation to copying the shape and the trend of the modulations, while using his own themes and rhythmical figures to carry out the design. The painter merely copies out another man's complete work. The composer writes his own work on the lines of his predecessor's model. Except to a heaven-born genius, such as Schubert, this system of studying form is the only possible one for the all-important control of shape and proportion. It might even, without blasphemy, be said that Schubert would have been less given to diffuseness if he had trained himself systematically, which we know that he did not; for his "heavenly lengths," as Schumann termed them, are only carried off by the wealth of invention which they contain. Beethoven often writes at as great a length as he (witness the Sonata in B flat, Op. 106), but his subjects, episodes, and developments all increase in proportion to each other and in proportion to the length of the scheme; and just as a man of perfect proportions will not look like a giant, even if he is six feet six, so another of six feet two, whose legs are too long for his body, will give the impression of abnormal height. It is an almost cruel task to write a movement, bar by bar, modulation by modulation, figure by figure, exactly the same in all respects, save theme, as a work by another composer; but it is the only way to get at the root of the matter, *and it must be faced.*

For the purpose of explaining how this practice can be systematically carried out, we will consider the first movement of Beethoven's Pianoforte Sonata, Op. 31, No. 3, and specify (I.) the ground proportions and (II.) the proportions of the details to each other, and their place in the whole scheme.

I. PROPORTIONS OF THE WHOLE MOVEMENT

First Subject . . . . 17 bars.
First Episode (bridge to second subject) . 28 bars.

(This includes what is sometimes termed a bye-subject, called a "Seiten-Thema" in Germany; a kind of second part to the theme proper.)

Second Subject . . . . 18 bars.
Second Episode . . . . 19 bars.
Codetta . . . . 6 bars.

(*N.B.* — The beginnings of the first episode, the second episode and the codetta are specimens of overlapping rhythm; the end of the one coinciding with the beginning of the next.)

This whole section is repeated.

Development . . . . 48 bars.
First Subject ⎫   17 bars.
First Episode | 16 bars.
Second Subject ⎬ Recapitulation . . . 20 bars.
Second Episode | 24 bars.
Codetta ⎭   9 bars.
Coda . . . . 34 bars.

Excluding the double counting of overlapping rhythms, the general broad proportions are as follows:

First Subject and its belongings . . 45 bars ⎫ 87.
Second Subject and its belongings . . 43 bars ⎭
Development . . . . 48 bars.
First Subject, etc. ⎫ Recapitulation   33 bars ⎫ 82.
Second Subject, etc. ⎭   50 bars ⎭
Coda . . . . 34 bars.

FORM 81

The first and second subjects balance each other.

The development is about one-half of the sum of the first and second subjects.

The recapitulation is slightly less than the first presentation of the first and second subjects.

The code is about three-fourths of the length of the development.

II. PROPORTIONS OF THE DETAILS

We have now to show the various divisions to which the copyist must work, using his own material and his own rhythms.

The first subject is a repeated theme of eight bars, with one extra bar to link them.

This eight-bar theme has three distinct rhythmical phrases :

A. ♩♪ ♩ ♩ | in the first bar, which is repeated exactly.

B. ♩ ♩ ♩ | ♩· | in the third and fourth bars, which is repeated with a difference of modulation and an ornamental (*i.e.* not essential) pause.

C. ♩♪ ♬♬♩ | ♩ in the seventh and eighth bars.

The connecting link is only a scale to take the repetition to a higher octave, having nothing to do with
Bars. the theme proper, with the exception of borrowing the start from the semiquaver figure in *C*; it does not disturb the balance, and is a kind of written-out pause

10. The theme is then repeated, but at different octaves

G

of the scale, so avoiding monotony and at once suggesting variation.

Bars.
17. The last note of the theme overlaps the beginning of the episode; the repeated bass carries out the idea of the long-repeated notes of B.

18.
19. } A treated with different modulations, altered intervals, and an added ornament.

20.
21. } A in the right hand treated in diminution by the method known as *ribattuta*, and the rhythm of B in the left hand combined with it.

22-25. The same phrase as 18-21, further varied by a shake taking the place of an ornament.

Bars 18-25 constitute the first of the three sections of the episode.

25, 26. The phrase-rhythms again overlap. The semiquavers of C become the kernel of a new two-bar phrase, partly florid, partly broken arpeggio.

27, 28. The same repeated, but the first bar varied.

29-32. The arpeggio figure developed throughout, the end of it repeated in *ribattuta*.

Bars 25-32 constitute the second section of the episode.

33, 34. A in the minor.

35, 36. B in the minor, but varied and intensified.

37-38.
39-40.
41-42. } B in different positions three times, so providing means for a modulation which will lead to the dominant.

42. A with an extended interval and with the rhythm ♫ ♩ modified to ♩ ♩.

43, 44. A becomes an octave leap, which is taken up and continued down to the bass.

Bars 33-45 constitute the third section of the episode.

FORM

Before analysing further we must note how Beethoven contrasts polyphony and monophony, or, to put it in the simplest language, where he harmonises his melodies and where he only suggests to the ear the chord on which his single-note and octave passages are based.

Bars   1–8.   Polyphony.
        8, 9.   Single notes.
     10–25.   Polyphony.
     25–32.   Single notes and octaves.
     33–44.   Polyphony.
     44, 45.   Single notes.

The relative contrast is 34 bars of polyphony to 11 of monophony. In addition, it will be noticed that he never uses more than one chord to a bar; when there appears to be more than one, the change is rather chromatic (as in bar 20) or melodic (as in bar 35). If a student first grounded in harmony were gifted enough to hit upon the theme of this sonata, he would in all probability treat it after this fashion:

The difference is one of darkness and light. In copying the model, therefore, adopt the same principles of harmonisation and contrast of unison and octave which it evidences.

Then, as to the modulation to the key of the dominant (B flat), in which the second subject is written, notice that by reaching it through a suggestion of its dominant (F major) he gives a definite foothold to the dominant when it appears; but, on the other hand, by his previous insistence upon the tonic through the first section, and his intensification of that insistence by using the tonic minor immediately before the modulation, he succeeds in making the dominant subordinate to the tonic, and never allows it to sound as if it were the real tonality of the piece. If he were to do so (and a student will find that it is only too easy to fall into this trap), the tonic, when it returned, would sound like the subdominant, and the tonality of the whole would be destroyed. To proceed with the analysis:

Bars. The second subject, again, is in two sections, the second being a very varied repetition of the first, and joined by a still longer link than were the two sections of the first subject. So it exactly balances the first in design, and intensifies that design. It has also three distinct rhythmical phrases:

45-53.   D. ♩. ♫♫ in the first bar, which is repeated in rhythm but not in position in the second bar.

E. ♫♫♫ in third and fourth bars. This is a throw-back to the *ribattuta* in bar 20.

FORM 85

Bars.
54-56.   F. ♪♪♪♪♪ (preceded by one bar of D) in a longer consecutive melody of four bars. The connecting link is four bars long instead of two in section 1.

57-64.   The second subject repeated, and the notes greatly varied by ornamental variations; the last note of the second subject is again the first of the second episode. Beethoven prevents the movement from getting into blocks, by dovetailing the rhythmical phrases into each other.

64, 65.   A combination of the linking scale (bars 8 and 53) with variations of the first bar of the second subject (bar 46), the rhythm D ♩. ♫♫ being converted into ♩ ♩.

66, 67.   64 and 65 repeated an octave higher.

68-71.   Bar 67 repeated with varying harmonies and movement. Also in cross rhythm $\frac{2}{4}$, crossing $\frac{3}{4}$.

Bars 64–71 constitute the first of the two sections of this episode.

72-74.
75-77.   A broken arpeggio of semiquavers, which settle down into quavers, and are related to 26.

78-81.   The arpeggio continues in the bass, and the shakes first hinted at in bar 65, repeated often in 68–71, become one long shake in the treble.

This is the second section of the episode.

82.   The beginning of the codetta synchronises with the end of the second episode; a connecting link recalling bar 9.

83, 84.   Two chords, A of the first theme, quieted down.

Bars.	
85.	A variation of *C* also quieted down.
86.	The connecting link repeated.
87, 88.	Repetition of 83, 84, with a different end to lead back to the repetition and to the tonic key. The end of the codetta is lopped of two bars in order to dovetail more completely into the next passage.

In this section of the first part the proportion of polyphony to monophony is 30 to 15.

DEVELOPMENT SECTION

89-92.	The first four bars of the sonata repeated, *A* and *B*.
93, 94.	*B* repeated, modulating.
95, 96.	*B* repeated, modulating further.
96-99.	A break, and a connecting link, founded on A, and being a written out version of the pause in bar 6.
100.	Bar 100 = bar 17.
101-108.	= bars 18-25, but in the relative minor.
108.	= bar 17.
109-113.	A threefold repetition of the figure

of bars 20, 21 (see *ante*), and a suggestion of the skip in A, reversed.

114, 115.	= bars 64, 65, modulating; the scale becoming an arpeggio as at 71.
116-121.	The section 108-115 is balanced by its repetition in following bars, but in another key.
122, 123. 124, 125. 126, 127.	All repetitions of 122, 123 in different keys, and providing means of modulation.
128-130.	The final bar of the phrase 122, 123 only (*ribattuta* repetition).
131-136.	The arpeggio figure of the bass in bar 123 used in

FORM

cross-rhythm, so as to gradually form the opening chord of the first subject.

The development may be divided into three sections:
1. Bars 89-108. A variant of portions of the first theme and first episode.
2. 108-122. Variants of the first episode and second episode.
3. 123-136. Variants of the second episode.

THE RECAPITULATION

Bars.
137-153. = 1-17. Note for note.
153-161. = 17-25. Bars 22, 23, and 24 only, varied in ornament.
161-169. A shortened version of 25-45, twelve bars being omitted. He continues the arpeggio of bar 31 an additional octave upwards, so as to land on B flat (the dominant) and bring the second subject into the tonic. He omits the minor version of the first subject 33-43, as it is no longer necessary to insist on the tonality (see above), and recapitulation generally gains by shortening. On the other hand, he sometimes individualises a recapitulation by lengthening and intensifying, very rarely leaving it exactly as it was in the first part.
170-190. = 46-64, lengthened by two bars, which are added to the connecting-link scale (compare bars 53-56 with bars 177-182), thereby increasing the pianistic brilliancy.
190-213. = 64-82, lengthened by five bars, four of which are added to the passage of cross-rhythm shakes (compare bars 68-71 with bars 194-201), and one added after the ascending arpeggios (compare 76, 77 with 206-208), the arpeggios themselves being reinforced.

Bars.	
213-219.	= 82–88. As on the first occasion the dominant led back to the tonic, here the tonic leads on to the subdominant (A flat), in which key the coda proper begins.
220-225.	The first subject, A and B only, with chromatic modu-
225-229.	lations. The last two chords only of B, treated in *ribattuta*, and continuing the chromatic modulation.
230-233.	B twice repeated and completing the modulation back to E flat.
234-236.	C and the connecting scale of bars 8 and 9, but chromatic throughout, and written in more rapid notes.
237-241.	A and B as at the beginning.
242, 243.	The last two chords of B repeated twice.
244, 245.	A brilliant passage, preserving the chromatic character of the coda, and finally clamping the modulation and fixing its finish in the tonic.
246-253.	The final passage; bars 246-249 are founded on bars 25-28 of the first episode, but treated in imitation, and varied as well, the closing passage being the broken arpeggio from the same source and related in shape to that at bars 72-75.

If this analysis is carefully followed, it will be especially noticeable that there is not one single bar of "padding." All the figures and passages have a logical origin in some detail of the themes. When the student writes a movement upon this or any other model, he had better work in another key, and in another tempo, $\frac{2}{4}$ instead of $\frac{3}{4}$, or $\frac{3}{4}$ instead of $\frac{2}{4}$; and if he adopts a minor mode for the copy of a model in the major mode, he will, of course, vary his contrasted keys accordingly. His rough rules in choosing this particular sonata (which he can afterwards modify to suit to any other model which he takes) are:

FORM

Make the phrases of the first subject contrast (as A, B and C do).

Keep the second subject as distinct in style and feeling from the first subject as possible, without losing the general character and atmosphere of the piece, and let its treatment be as well contrasted as itself. The look of it on the paper alone will be a test of contrast. The first subject of this sonata is mainly in notes of longer value, the second of shorter value, as a glance at the first two pages will show. One of Beethoven's frequent methods of contrasting the two subjects will be of great service; when his first subject is written on a *scale* melody, his second subject is frequently written on a *chord* melody, and *vice versa*. The C Minor Symphony is an excellent example of this:

in complete contrast with each other, the one on a chord, the other on a scale; the one *staccato*, the other *legato*; the one fierce, the other gentle; but each related to the other by the little phrase (*a*).

Do not write irrelevant passages (which are padding), *however pleasing or brilliant.* Found them on some basis in your themes. Oak leaves do not grow on beeches. Your compositions must be like a tree, consistent in character from the roots below the ground to the topmost branches, and clothed with foliage which is at once homogeneous to itself and to the tree from which it springs.

Treat your modulations so as to lead to the key to which you are modulating without anticipating its entry.

This is one of the most common traps of the inexperienced writer. He knocks at the door of his host and runs away, because he finds that he is a few minutes before his time. This anticipation of the entry of a new key, or of a return to the original one, discounts all the charm and freshness of the key when it comes. It is often quite advisable to use the *minor* of the tonic to approach the tonic when the composition is in a major key, but not to use the major of the tonic to approach the tonic when it is in a minor key.

It is very important, for this radical reason, to avoid treating the tonic key *as the tonic* in the development section; the recapitulation will inevitably produce a feeling of monotony unless this sound common-sense rule is followed. If the tonic is used there at all it should be as a step in modulating elsewhere, such as to the subdominant.

Be as careful of the internal proportions of the development section as of the form of the whole scheme. It should have its climax and the subsidence after the climax on a small scale, just as the whole movement has on a large scale. There should always be a point of rest in it, which will give time to recover breath for the recapitulation.

Never repeat a phrase consecutively in exactly the same notes, unless you have a definite reason for wishing to hammer it in.

FORM

This is a trap which caught so many Mendelssohn lovers in the last century. There are very few composers, just as there are very few men, who have not some tricks which grow upon them unawares and become often unduly accentuated; and as these tricks are more noticeable than more solid qualities, they are the more apt to attract the attention and to become absorbed in the memory of a receptive brain. Of all tricks the meaningless repetition of a phrase is one of the most wearisome. Variation power will be the best antidote. Repetition is one of the most valuable assets of a composer, but he must guard against its abuse; he must copy its perfections and not its imperfections. It can be as strongly, perhaps even more strongly, employed through the agency of rhythm than through that of melody.

In writing a minuet, or any short piece in that form, remember that the portion after the double bar and before the return must be as interesting as the first part.

This is too frequently neglected, just for the reason that the second part is the most difficult to write. A tyro will more or less exhaust his inventive power in the first part, and find himself gravelled after he has stated his theme. This is because the athletic training of his brain is only just beginning. The powers of contrast and development, musically interesting in themselves, will come as the training progresses, and it is only by trying hard, and by ruthlessly rejecting what he finds unsuitable or inadequate, that this training will become complete. The composer, in a word, is his own trainer; the teacher can only make suggestions as to the direction and scope of the training.

MUSICAL COMPOSITION

Write in the style of whatever instrument you are writing for, and remember its compass. For this reason it is wiser for a beginner (at all events after he has made a fair start) to avoid writing for the instrument which he is most accustomed to play. An organist composer will gain much more benefit from writing for the piano or the strings than by writing for the organ; though he will find it very difficult at first to accustom himself to florid passage writing, or to an instrument such as the piano, which, on the one hand, is incapable of sustaining a note at the same power throughout its length, and which, on the other hand, can produce a sense of dynamic rhythm, accent and phrasing which the organ can only hint at. All are safe in writing for strings, if only for the reason that they play in the pure scale; but a string player who composes will be greatly handicapped if he is not at home in writing for a keyed instrument as well. A pianoforte player or an organist who is unacquainted with violin technique can very speedily find the way of writing suitably for it by studying violin music, and by losing no opportunity of listening to it and getting the style, sound and colour of it into his system. The first tendency of the composer of piano music (especially if he is an organist or violinist) is to write wholly and solely in the middle three octaves of the instrument, a habit which is still further encouraged if he begins his training with a long course of harmony exercises. He must remember the seven-octave range, and he will be surprised at the contrasts of pitch which it provides so easily. (Compare bars 10–15 of the sonata analysed above.) When the student has thoroughly grasped all this groundwork and practised writing in extended

FORM

sonata form, first by following some models closely, and afterwards by writing independently on an average basis of all the models he has followed, he will be able, with certainty of touch and without loss of symmetry, to adapt the form to the requirements of his inventions, and to introduce various modifications of shape, such as the omission of some episode, the shortening or lengthening of a development, the omission or inclusion of a coda, while preserving the balance of the whole design. But this he must work up to through a drudgery as great as any other profession or art demands, if he is to reach anything approaching perfection in it, and to make any valuable impression on the ears which listen to his compositions.

Assuming that the composer has now thoroughly mastered technique and form, and is at home in the varied treatment of rhythmical phrases, what is his next step? *To forget all about them.* They will take care of themselves. They are firmly fixed in the system, and the brain, which has been so far ridden on the curb, must now be ridden on the snaffle. It is the composer's own responsibility to take up the curb rein at any moment when he finds himself unable to surmount some technical difficulty, or when he discovers a flaw in his own equipment. But when he once begins independent inventive work, he must put his technical rules behind him, just as a painter forgets his rules of perspective and mixes his colours unconsciously. He has been through his term of slavery and won his freedom. Neither he nor any one else will appreciate the full joys of his freedom if he is always harping back on his slavery. Freedom means life to music, but only when it is won by genuine hard work.

Freedom which is not so won will inevitably degenerate into licence. There is no royal road to it except through blood and tears.

> "Wer nie sein Brod mit Thränen ass,
> Wer nie die kummervollen Nächte
> Auf seinem Bette weinend sass,
> Der kennt euch nicht, ihr himmlischen Mächte!"

CHAPTER VII

COLOUR

TONE-COLOUR, which for the sake of abbreviation we shall term simply colour, is the dress in which we clothe the flesh and bones which constitute the living body of music. The body is for all time, and any changes which it undergoes are imperceptibly slow. The clothes are for a fraction of time, and vary with the taste and fashion of that fraction; they are simple where life is simple, and tend to become more elaborate as the craftsmanship of their manufacturers improves, and as the wealth and luxury of their wearers increase. Fine feathers are said to make fine birds, but the proverb somewhat smacks of satire; for neither the peacock nor the cock-pheasant is remarkable for beauty of voice, nor the toucan for beauty of proportion; while the comparative dowdiness of an eagle cannot conceal the nobility and beauty of its shape, and the voice of a drab-coloured nightingale or plain brown thrush will give more joy to the ear than all the magnificence of a peacock's tail will to the eye. In the bird-world Nature seems to divide her favours; to gorgeous plumage she denies beauty of voice, to beauty of voice she denies gorgeous plumage. In the world of art she is kinder, for a painting can make its appeal both by its beauty of line, its subject, its perfection of draughtsmanship, and by its mastery of colour as well. A musical composition can do the same. But as the bird with beauty of voice will always touch the hearts of mankind more than the bird with beauty of plumage, and no man would hesitate as to which he would choose to live with, so the beauty of melodies and of the perfect treatment of them will always live longer and accord more with the natural sympathies of man than volumes of prismatic sound devoid of pure melody or finished workmanship. Excessively brilliant colour may temporarily blind the eye and deafen the ear to deficiencies in both, but sooner or later it will pall, and the underlying faults and failures will become more and more evident. It is always a sound test of a picture to photograph it, and of an orchestral piece to arrange it for a monochrome instrument such as the pianoforte. If the musical work is beautiful in melody, finished in detail, and well-balanced in design, the cold arrangement on what von Bülow termed a "box of hammers" will give as much pleasure in its limited scope as a photograph or an engraving of a masterpiece of Velasquez or of Bellini. We shall miss "the top-dressing" and no more. A composition which relies primarily or solely on its orchestral colour will be intolerable when reduced to black and white. No musician can honestly say that the greater part of Berlioz' work gives real pleasure when it is played in a pianoforte arrangement, while even the most complicated and highly-coloured pages of the *Nibelungen*, of the *Meistersinger*, or of *Tristan* will stand the test

COLOUR

triumphantly, in spite of the omissions which the limitation of ten fingers imposes.

What, then, is colour in music? The term has really a twofold meaning. There is, firstly, colour in the sense of variety of expression, and of the timbre or quality of sound which underlies that variety in a single instrument. Complete command of all varieties of colour—as distinct from tone gradations—is the almost exclusive possession of the human voice: instruments only possess it within limits. The pianoforte does not possess it at all except by the mechanical contrivance of the soft and damper pedals; the violin can only get it by the use of a mute, or by pizzicato with the fingers; the harp only by harmonics. Some wind instruments possess it to a greater or less extent, such as the high, medium and low registers of the flute, clarinet and bassoon. The horn with its round soft notes and its brassed (cuivré) quality. The voice can be round, nasal, rough, smooth, declamatory and whispering as the emotions indicated by the words require, and this kind of colour, which we will term "individual," is only to be attained on mechanically made instruments to a very modified extent. The only quality in the instrumental player which can give an impression of its existence is what is termed "temperament."

The other kind of colour we shall term "collective." It is produced by combinations of the timbre of different instruments and their contrast to each other; and the only keyed instrument which possesses in itself the capacity of collective colour is the organ, by means of its various stops and wind-pressures. Individual colour is the sole property of the executive artist; the composer has no control over it on paper. Collective colour is the sole property of the composer, and the executive artist has no control over it on paper. He can spoil the effect of the composer's colouring by inferior playing, but he cannot alter its inherent qualities. The picture may be hung in a bad light, but its value remains the same. Lack of temperament and sense of colour in a singer will hurt him more than it will harm a song. It is with "collective" colour, therefore, that we have here to deal; with the means of producing it, of regulating the amount of its use, and the variety and contrast which it places at the composer's disposal. It is used in three main lines of composition, concerted music, orchestral music, and music for instruments and voices, solo and choral, with or without scenic adjuncts. In concerted music we have it in sonatas for pianoforte and a solo instrument (such as the violin or violoncello or a wind-instrument), in trios, quartets and quintets for similar combinations, in pieces for solo wind instruments and strings, and in concertos for a solo instrument with orchestral accompaniment. In orchestral music such as overtures, symphonies and ballet music. In combination with voices such as oratorios, cantatas and operas.

I. ORCHESTRATION

In order to be able to deal with colour at all, a student must first study the capabilities, character *and the limitations* of any instrument in use. He will find ample means of proper information on this subject in the numerous treatises on orchestration which are now ready to his hand, such as those by Berlioz, Gevaert, Prout, Widor and others. But he must not rely solely upon any one of them, except as regards the purely technical definitions of each instrument. When he comes to study the combinations of instruments, he had better compare them all and pick out the plums for himself.

A tyro who exclusively studies Berlioz, for example, will risk falling into his peculiar and individual methods of instrumentation, and will very soon exaggerate all his peculiarities and more striking oddities, instead of giving greater attention to the main lines of common sense, of which his book is full. An experienced master will recognise in a moment the score of a composer who has founded his methods exclusively upon Berlioz. He taught most modern composers what they did not know before, or only knew intuitively and without method; but the composer ought to choose his own lines of taste, while never neglecting to use any information he can get from him. Wagner undoubtedly sucked his brains, but it would be absurd to say that his orchestration was in any way a reflection of the Frenchman's. As a text-book it has the small defects of its great qualities. It is almost too picturesque; and the sparks of descriptive genius which light up almost every page are apt to blind the young reader to the essentially solid facts which constitute the main strength of the book. The analytical mastery of Gevaert's and Widor's treatises, and the concentrated essence of Prout's, may be a little less attractive, but they are safer ground upon which to begin delving. Books, however, only give the same idea of orchestration that a Baedeker or a Murray guide does of scenery. The maps and plans are useful, but give no clue to the contours and colours of a landscape, or to the architectural aspects of a city. Orchestration treatises, after they have explained the compasses of the various instruments, their mechanism, general character, capabilities and incapabilities, have said all they can say. All the discussions upon the quality of their sound, individually and collectively, are of no possible use to any one who has not heard them with his own ears. They may help the student's judgment and explain his difficulties after he is acquainted with the sounds they are discussing, but not before. It is safe to say that no musician who had never heard an orchestra could write a page of passable scoring with the help of books. His best and his only master is the orchestra itself, and his soundest method of studying it consists in frequent attendance at orchestral rehearsals, with the full scores of the works to be rehearsed in his hand. Rehearsals are best, because he will have more opportunity of hearing complex passages repeated, of analysing the quality of individual instruments, and of moving about so as to hear the orchestra from different positions; both close to it (and if possible above it, where he can dissect the sound), and at a distance, where he will get the general effect. It does not matter if the orchestra is small in numbers; indeed, for his purpose, it is better that it should be. Only in this way will the colour effects produced by the orchestra, in whole and in part, get firmly fixed in that part of his brain which can hear mentally while reading a score.

In the first efforts of composition it is a matter of necessity to start simply, as all the great masters did,

COLOUR 101

when the experience is small; not attempting to begin where Beethoven or Wagner left off, but working up through simplicity to a complexity which will be natural because it is not forced. The same holds true of orchestration. What a century evolved in its development, each composer must evolve in miniature for himself; beginning with the materials of Mozart, and on the basis of his incomparable method, adding by degrees to his materials, and elaborating them with the help of the subsequent mechanical improvements and inventions which have been made since his day. In indicating the plan which the student should follow, we shall assume that he has listened to orchestras, and knows the compass and character of the instruments. His first step should be one which involves considerable drudgery and manual labour, in return for which he will be taking lessons from masters greater than any he will be able to procure or to pay, and which are at his hand for the asking without travelling further than the shelves of his own library: Mozart, Beethoven and Wagner. He will begin by taking lessons from Mozart. If he has listened with a careful and critical ear to some of that master's orchestral compositions, he will have noticed the main principles upon which he works, and the nature of the materials which he has at his command. He must adopt both the principles and the limited means. To take the materials first: flutes, oboes, clarinets (in C, B flat, A), bassoons, drums, violins, violas, violoncellos and double basses are practically as at the present day. Not so the horns and trumpets, which, being the natural instruments without valves or slides, must only be given those notes to play which they can produce. On the other hand, the crooks whereby they can change their key must be chosen suitably to the key of the movement they play, so as to give them the maximum of scope; the particular quality given individually by the crooks themselves must also be known and weighed. The difference of tone-colour in the various crooks is not so marked in the trumpet as it is in the horn, and sufficient stress is not laid in the treatises upon this most important but very subtle distinction of quality. Even in the modern orchestra, where nearly everything, unfortunately, is played upon the F horn, that laziness has involved great loss of colour in the music written for the natural horn with crooks. In Beethoven's Symphony, No. 7, it is practically impossible even nowadays to play the horn parts except upon the very characteristic A crook; but his Eroica Symphony is usually played on the F horn instead of the E flat, for which it is written, with the result that the pile of the velvet is scraped off. A student of Wagner's full scores will notice that the crooks of the horn parts are constantly changed to suit the tonality of the passage in which they occur. Whether the printed directions of the composer are attended to or not is no concern of his. His experience of the various colours will only be gained by asking a friendly horn-player to play a given passage on the different crooks. His practice in writing for the instrument must tally with that of the player. Every good horn-player is trained at first on the natural horn without the use of valves. His ear will thus get accustomed to the roundness of tone which is so essential to its character, and he will endeavour to preserve the same quality when he adds the valves.

COLOUR   103

Composers will learn the best way to use the horns in a score by writing first with the cramped series of notes of the natural horn, and making up for its deficiencies by ingenuity of treatment, and even by inventing subjects which will minimise them. When he advances to writing with valve-horns he will not overstep the limits of true horn quality even in the most complex passages. The instruments he will begin by using are:

Wood.	1 or 2 Flutes. 2 Oboes. 2 Clarinets. 2 Bassoons.
Brass.	2 Horns. 2 Trumpets.
Percussion.	2 Kettle Drums.
Strings.	Violins (divided into firsts and seconds). Violas. Violoncellos. Double Basses.

Then as to the general principles of orchestral design. He will lay out the treatment on the lines of three parts and not four; for a study of Mozart will show that he distributes his parts in threes or multiples of three, a principle which Wagner elaborated in his later works by tripling each branch of the wood-wind family. This division of three applies to the contrasts and combinations of wood, brass and strings as well as to the general lie of the music itself. It is the true basis of all good instrumentation. Four-part treatment there will be, and plenty of it, but in a secondary position to three-part. For example, Mozart will more often group his strings thus:

I. Violin }	. . .	treble part.
II. Violin }		
Viola	. . .	tenor part.
'Cello }	. . .	bass part.
Bass }		

than thus:

I. Violin	. . .	treble part.
II. Violin	. . .	alto part.
Viola	. . .	tenor part.
'Cello }	. . .	bass part.
Bass }		

He would be more likely to lay out the common chord in E flat thus:

(It should be clearly understood that we are speaking of three-part grouping rather than of three-part harmony.)

Other general features which will strike the eye are:

(a) The tendency of wind-instruments to sustain chords.

(b) The reservation of cumulative treatment for extra force.

(c) The tendency of the double bass to move rather than to sustain notes (a held note on that instrument being necessarily unsatisfactory throughout its length excepting in soft passages), and to play in the upper octaves of its register rather than in the lower.

Bearing these points in mind, Mozart can give a most effective lesson in the following way. Buy a full score (say) of the Symphony in E flat, and a good full arrangement of it for pianoforte (four hands). Write the exact number of instruments and the keys and crooks of the clarinets, horns, trumpets and drums on lines corresponding to those of Mozart's printed score; and then instrument the Symphony for yourself from the pianoforte arrangement (without peeping into the original for the solution of any difficulties). Look with an orchestral eye at passages which are changed in order to adapt them to pianoforte technique, and reverse the process. After you have scored (say) the introductory adagio, copy the Mozart score *over your own and on the same lines as your own* in red ink, omitting, of course, all identical notes, and enabling you to compare *in situ* the differences between his work and yours. It is of no use to trust merely to comparison; the Mozart notes must be actually written down over your own, if this method of training is to do real good. When you have written it out, think over the differences between your work and his, and why his way is likely to sound better than yours. Repeat this process every thirty-two bars or so. When you begin you will be aghast at the differences; but as you continue and gradually absorb the style, you will be equally surprised at the rapidity with which the two scores assimilate. Do not lose sight of the necessity of writing horns and trumpets on the open notes only,

and lay out the passages in such a way as not to show the weak points of your machinery. For example, as low E flat  is below the compass of the double bass, do not write

but

The first will accentuate its limitations, the second will sound natural. Remember that the two most dangerous instruments in the orchestra are the double bass and the drums; the former in consequence of its lack of sustaining power, which prevents it taking the place or in any way reproducing the effect of organ pedals (too often used as its model and prototype), and of its hollow quality in the lower notes; the latter because its too frequent use drowns detail more than any other instrument, and induces monotony from the very qualities which make it so useful in accentuating colour. Remember that violoncellos supply a perfectly adequate and sonorous bass without any double basses at all, and that the double basses are only an adjunct to them in this capacity for purposes of reinforcement and not *vice versa*. Do not forget that the single notes of each of the wind parts represent the sound given by one instrument only, but that the single notes given to each of string parts represent the sound of several instruments; and, therefore, that the balance which the eye sees in reading the score has to be adjusted by the consideration that the five staves of wind are played by 10 players and the five staves of strings by any number from 25 to (say) 46 or 60. Lastly, remember that additional power in the wind is gained rather by doubling at the first and second octaves than by doubling at the unison: the reinforcement of the overtones producing more resonance than that of the fundamental note. This law of sound can be tested by any organist who compares the combination of two eight-foot open diapasons with that of one eight-foot diapason and a four-foot principal.

The E Flat Symphony omits a second flute and the oboes. The G Minor Symphony of which one version omits the clarinets and the other includes them, and which also has parts for two horns in different crooks, is for these reasons a most valuable study.

The student can first score it without clarinets and afterwards add them (excising some of the oboe parts where the clarinets are more suitable), and compare his addition and subtraction with Mozart's.

The Finale of the C Major Symphony (usually called the "Jupiter" in this country) is an excellent lesson in the orchestral treatment of fugue. The slow movements of all three are most instructive in contrast and what has been rightly termed the "conversation" of the instruments.

Before passing from Mozart, the student is strongly advised to apply the same system of study to some specimens of his orchestral accompaniments of vocal music. The following are useful examples: the song, "Deh vieni, non tardar" from *Figaro*; the recitative and aria "In quali eccessi" and the sestet "Sola, Sola" from *Don Giovanni*. The attempts to amplify the very meagre pianoforte arrangements of these pieces into orchestral form will be found easier after a good grounding in the symphonies. From Mozart, he can move on to Beethoven, and as he gets more at home in the work, he can confine himself to fragments of movements which seem the least easy or the most suggestive of variant colours; such as the slow movement of Symphony No. 4, the opening of the Finale of No. 5 (for sonorous, as opposed to noisy, *fortissimo*), the slow movement of No. 6, the Scherzo and Trio of No. 7, and the Allegretto of No. 8. He can try some experiments with Weber (Freischütz and Euryanthe overtures), and finally with Wagner, whose Siegfried-Idyll is a unique specimen of the maximum of effect attained by the simplest means, and any page or pages in the *Meistersinger*. This last score is supremely valuable to the student of orchestration if only for its economical and perfectly proportionate use of that dangerous rogue-elephant, the double bass.

A course of study of this plan will soon lead the student not only to assign a phrase to the instrument which suits it best, but even to get inspiration for his phrases from the tone-quality of the instrument which is in his mind. It will also teach him, in a way which no original experiments can, how to make his middle parts not only interesting in themselves but sufficiently full (without being overloaded) to balance the superstructure and the substructure. The texture of the middle part is the most troublesome to a beginner, and the most frequent cause of failure in the early stages; its insufficiency will make a work sound all top and bottom, and its over-elaboration will fog the general design. Due proportion will only be reached after many a failure, which will bring the drops of a miserable perspiration out of the brow of the composer as he writhes under hearing it. But he can console himself with the knowledge that all his predecessors have gone through the same experience, and can read Berlioz' graphic account of his own sufferings on a like occasion. The tendency of the present day to add to the wind-instruments in numbers and in quality, to write horn parts which are merely a filling up of the harmonies without regard to their suitability to the instrument, and to subdivide the strings into a great number of parts, is a matter of grave question. Its main result is to produce in the listener the same feeling of monotony which he feels after listening to an organ recital exclusively given upon the full swell, with the closing and opening of the shutters for its only means of gradation.

The full swell is a fascinating sound, and so is the richness of a densely-populated modern orchestra. But if one or other is to get full value for its effect, it must be used as a contrast only, and a rare contrast too. No one knew this better than Wagner did. The first act of the *Walküre* alone is sufficient to prove it. He used his horns with great chromatic freedom, but never for padding, and never with disregard of their *timbre*. He subdivided his violins, but never allowed the wind-instruments to take advantage of their scattered numbers and wipe them out. He used his extra instruments, such as the cor anglais, bass clarinet, double bassoon, tuba, *et hoc genus omne*, not to fill up a general clatter and to add extra notes, but as exponents of passages which were written for and required their particular type of colour. When he aims at an effect of confusion (such as the coming of the swan in *Lohengrin*, or, still more, the street row in the *Meistersinger*) he arrives at complexity through simplicity. Every part in itself runs naturally and satisfactorily to the player. The result is that it all (to use a common but descriptive phrase) "comes off."

This mastery he owed, as he would himself have been the first to admit, to his complete knowledge of Mozart, Beethoven and Weber. The so-called modern type of full-swell instrumentation owes nothing to any of them. It is only the natural result of revelling too much in Wagner's *climaxes* of polyphonic sound, which he used economically, and with which the less experienced of his successors gamble. The charm of individual conversation between the instruments, of which Schubert was so great a master, is for the moment abolished. Why? Because in many cases the instruments have nothing to say. There is just material enough for a buzz of general conversation, but no talker sufficiently interesting to arrest the attention of the other talkers. The invention is, therefore, in inverse ratio to the colour, and the richness of colour is used to conceal the poverty of invention. It often succeeds, momentarily; but when the trick is found out the failure will be proportionately greater. The palette of a painter is a beautiful study of colour, both simple and complex; but he would not exhibit it as a picture

COLOUR

unless he was qualifying for Bedlam. He knows, as every sane and sound composer knows, that it is only a secondary means to a primary end. It is the clothes of his subject. As the old masters drew all their figures nude, and added the draperies after their figures were perfected, so the composer's colour should be the "high lights" which illuminate the beauty of his melodic invention and of his perfection of detail. The fading of Sir Joshua Reynolds' pigments has not destroyed the beauty of his designs or the charm of his conceptions. But if he had relied mainly on his perishable colours, and scamped his drawing, his pictures would have been long ago relegated to oblivion. Colour is a first-rate servant, but a very insidiously bad master.

II. CHAMBER AND CONCERTED MUSIC

In chamber music it is still less possible to rely on colour as superior to design. It bears the same relation to orchestral treatment that water-colours do to oils. The texture and the mediums are thinner, and flaws of workmanship are all the more obvious. But in music the mastery of the one is essential to the mastery of the other. The writing of a trio or quartet for solo stringed instruments is the best possible training for the treatment of the body of strings in the orchestra. It will teach the composer (1) how much more richness can be obtained from a chord of four notes in a string quartet than from the same chord on the pianoforte; (2) how little is to be gained by unnecessary and superfluous doubling; (3) how to secure contrast with very limited material; (4) how much harm can be done by a single ill-fitting note (even of semiquaver value); (5) how to attain complete freedom in the relation of the four instruments to each other; (6) how to make all four parts equally interesting to the players. Much variety of actual colour is not possible of attainment in a string quartet, but each of the three instruments which compose it, the violin, viola and violoncello, has an individuality of its own: the violin the thinnest but the most brilliant, the viola the roundest and possessing more of the "larmes au voix," the violoncello the most nasal and incisive in the upper registers, and the most dignified and sonorous in the lower. (Their counterparts in the wind family are the oboe, clarinet, horn and bassoon). Their range is great, far too great for the harmony-exercise student to grasp with any ease, and their interweaving powers are almost illimitable. The colour of the whole combination will completely change when the violoncello or the viola ascend above their brethren in giving out a theme, as the following examples from Beethoven's quartet in E flat, Op. 127, will show:

or if passages are distributed in *pizzicato*, separately or together; or if mutes are used in any or all of the parts. The student can profitably find out many examples for himself. The main principle to grasp in string-quartet writing is the importance of providing plenty of rests. A quartet might almost answer to the Irishman's description of a net, as a "lot of holes held together by a string." A kind of rough criticism may be applied to it by investigating whether the parts provide sufficient opportunities for the players to turn over the leaves with ease. If they have to omit a passage in order to turn, or to provide themselves with a friend to do it for them, it is pretty certain that the quartet is deficient in the valuable contrast afforded by rests. To return to the six points of advantage to the composer mentioned above, and consider them separately.

(1) The richness of a combination of four strings is due partly to the quality and number of overtones, and partly to the fact that they play in the pure scale. Even when only one or two parts are employed, they will sound much more satisfying to the ear than when they are played upon the pianoforte, and the addition of other parts will not only double, but square and cube the richness.

(2) As to unnecessary or superfluous doubling. It is well known that the sound of a single violin is far preferable to that of two violins playing in unison, and that it is not till the number reaches at least four that the collective effect in unison is satisfactory. Any doubling, therefore, in a quartet must necessarily produce this unsatisfactory colour. If there is any doubling at all, it should come either from the natural run of the parts and be transitory, or be given to the two instruments least alike in quality, such as the 'cello and the violin, or be restricted to passages in octaves. But in a composition so limited in its means, a rest is better than a doubling, and no notes should be thrown away.

COLOUR 115

(3) The methods of contrast have been sufficiently hinted at above.

(4) The perfection of every note in a quartet, and the necessity of putting it in its proper place even to a fraction is one of the axioms of good workmanship. It does not avail to excuse an ugly or unsuitable note by pleading the rapidity with which it goes by. The same ear which will instantly detect the clerical omission of a sharp or a flat ought to train itself to correct ruthlessly an incongruous note, or an ill-fitting rhythmical figure. Purity of style depends upon this rigid self-criticism, and without purity of style it is better that chamber music should not exist. The danger is that a composer's ear may accustom itself to like what is really an ugliness because it has heard it so often, and is prejudiced in its favour by belonging to the person who wrote it. That the human being can accustom his palate even to enjoy cod-liver oil or a superannuated egg is a well-known fact; but he has only degenerated his tasting power, and port for the average man remains preferable as a drink to castor oil. The best remedy for this not uncommon disease is the advice of an experienced friend. In most cases a harsh or unexpected note or figure will pass muster if the writer has a definite logical reason for writing it which he can clearly explain. If it cannot be defended by such means, it generally spells carelessness and bad workmanship.

(5) It is needless perhaps to point out that the road to complete freedom in the treatment of the four instruments lies through counterpoint. The run of each part pertains to design. Colour comes in when the characteristics of each instrument are kept in view

in the relation it bears to its colleagues, and when the variations of position, high and low, close and spread, are taken full advantage of. No better examples of characteristic relation can be quoted than the examples from Beethoven given above. What is meant by variation of position the following ways of treating the common chord of C will illustrate:

An interesting example (shown on the opposite page) from Beethoven's quartet (Op. 59, No. 1) will show how strong effects of colour can be produced by this means.

One more point must be kept in mind under this heading: the vital importance of putting down as accurately as possible on paper the degrees of force, variations of tone, bowing, slurs, *legato* and *staccato* marks, and changes of time which the composer intends. He must not trust to the taste or intelligence of any one but himself, if he wishes his work to be

heard as he intends it to sound. This rule applies to all music, and especially to orchestral and chamber music. No executant can be expected to look at a passage as if the brains of the writer had been temporarily transferred to him. An inexperienced composer often thinks that no player could possibly interpret his work except in the way he thinks of it himself, and he omits to write down definite directions for his guidance. There have, it is true, been executants and conductors of genius who seem intuitively to know the intentions of a composer without any assistance from him at all. But von Bülows are few and far between. He must not expect to find them growing on every bush. He must legislate for the musician of average capability and leave nothing to chance. A *crescendo* and *diminuendo*, an *sf*, a sudden *pianissimo*, may alter the whole character of a passage, and turn dulness into brilliancy. A slight *ritenuto* or *accelerando* may make a phrase lilt, when without them it hangs fire. A violin passage carelessly bowed may destroy a rhythm. He must be careful also to describe the pace of his movements in the right terms, and if possible to verify them by hearing them played before he fixes it finally; for a work, when it comes to be performed, often demands a different *tempo* from what the composer has imagined in his head, and this experience is still more necessary to a beginner, who not infrequently changes the pace in his mind, unconsciously, as he writes. There is an abundance of terms whereby he can indicate pace without tying it down irretrievably with a metronome mark, but he must be accurate in his choice of them. Mistakes most frequently arise in slow movements, where he will often write *lento* when he means *andante,* or *andante* when he means *adagio.* The metronome is only of use as indicating the mean average to which the pace should conform without being inelastic; and even that average is liable to change when the exigencies of a large or small room demand it.

The composer is strongly recommended to adhere to Italian as the universal language of music signs. It has in recent times become a sort of mock-patriotic fad of his to write directions in the language of his own country, which would be all very well if his music were only performed there; but his patriotism stops short of any desire to confine it to his native land. Every player and singer in every country understands Italian terms. The difficulties which Englishmen experience when they are faced with such German terms as "nicht schleppend," "noch rascher," "innig"

COLOUR

may be appreciated by imagining what a German player would make of such phrases as "keep the lilt," "without slackening," "with marked emphasis," and such like. The only practical result of such imbecility is that the players, not having a dictionary in their pockets, neglect the instructions altogether. The faddists, who amuse themselves in setting these linguistic problems to men who have enough to do as it is with tackling the music itself, are not even consistent, for their pages are full of *p* (=piano), *f* (=forte), *crescendo*, *dim.* (=diminuendo), and so on; Italian terms on every line. A firm stand should be made in the interests of the universal language, music, against such accentuations of the mischief wrought at the Tower of Babel. It is better for a composer to risk a few mistakes in Italian grammar than have his work inadequately performed because his directions are not intelligible. As French is the accepted language in diplomacy, so Italian should be in music. One can well imagine the blank and nonplussed astonishment of a Western conductor and his executants if they found that all the directions in the scores and parts of Russian, Hungarian or Bohemian composers were only given in Slavonic or Magyar.

(6) To make the parts equally interesting to all the players, it is necessary (*a*) to conform to the technique of the instruments, and so write gratefully for them; (*b*) to let each part run in its own path, and be as melodically complete in itself as it is possible to make it. This is the secret of a quartet sounding well and "coming off," as it is also in an orchestral piece. Crabbed writing produces crabbed sounds. A touch or two may make a difficult passage easy and clear up

a whole phrase. No music gains in the hearing by being made purposely difficult. Difficulties in reason there must be, but only where it is certain that the passage cannot, by a few alterations, be made to sound as well in a more practicable shape.

All these considerations apply with equal force to other forms of chamber music. In string trios the standard must be three parts, and not a mongrel four secured by perpetual double-stopping in the various instruments. This type of composition, if imagined and carried out upon a genuine three-part basis, will be of great value as a training for the orchestral writing of strings. A study of such a work as the C Minor Trio of Beethoven (Op. 9, No. 3) will be invaluable.

The first four bars of it

are enough to show that the composition is thought out for three parts and no more. The impression of richness is gained (as in the second and third bars above) rather by arpeggio than by chord. There is no lack of double-stoppings in the work, but they are almost always on a basis of three parts (like Mozart's orchestra), such as the first bars after the repeat in the first movement, which are a harmonisation of the unison in the example above:

which is answered at once by an accentuation of three parts only,

a passage which does not sound at all the thinner or poorer for its juxtaposition to thicker harmonies.

In all other respects this type belongs in its methods of treatment to the string quartet, while its limitations afford an excellent antidote to the danger of writing orchestrally for solo strings. One maxim ought to be kept steadily in mind in both. Avoid quick reiterated notes (or tremolo) such as  unless you want it for a very special effect (such as Brahms used in the slow movement of the clarinet quintet). In ninety-nine cases out of a hundred, a well-designed semiquaver figure, or passage will be far more interesting both to player and to hearer, and will preserve the quartet atmosphere. When one or more solo wind instruments are used in chamber music, the principle is the same as that given above in (6) and elsewhere. Forget the orchestra, and remember that the balance of parts is wholly different from that of the orchestra, there being only one player to each string part.

The best models for combined wind and strings are the clarinet quintets of Mozart and of Brahms, the septet of Beethoven, and the octet of Schubert. When the pianoforte enters into the scheme the conditions greatly alter, and the writing for the strings becomes in some ways more hampered and more difficult. There is a basis of quarrel between them at the start, for the pianoforte is tuned in the tempered scale, where every interval except the octave is out of tune, and the strings play in the pure scale. This quarrel has to be smoothed over temporarily when they join forces, and the causes of friction have to be avoided as much as it is possible to avoid them. The accomplished violinist or violoncellist will adapt himself at critical moments to the cast-iron requirements of the pianoforte, but the occasions when he has to accomplish this difficult *volte-face* must be minimised by the experience and common sense of the composer. He ought, for instance, to avoid giving the stringed instrument passages of melody in unison with the keyed, assigning them to another octave if they require reinforcement, and generally keeping the string part as independent as possible both in figure and in phrase.

The basis of a sonata for piano and violin of the type adopted by Mozart and Beethoven, and continued with modifications and enrichments down to our own day, is a three-part one, distributed as follows:

   I. Violin,   or   I. Piano, right hand,
 II. Piano, right hand,   II. Violin,
III. Piano, left hand,   III. Piano, left hand,

and occasionally even (when the piano is played in the higher registers):

   I. Piano, right hand,
 II. Piano, left hand,
III. Violin.

The best models are Mozart, Beethoven, Brahms, and, as a very striking specimen of independent development of the style, César, Franck.

The trio for pianoforte, violin and 'cello is also on a three-part basis, but differently distributed:

   I. Violin,
 II. 'Cello,
III. Pianoforte, both hands,

and also interchangeable. An element of great importance comes in here. The strings belong to one family of colour wholly distinct from that of the piano, and, while each separately can play the same rôle with it as in the sonata, their tone-affinity demands that when they both play together their two-part exposition must be as complete and satisfactory as that of two singers in a duet. It will not do for them merely to fill up the missing notes of a chord, or to play phrases which, if the pianoforte part were omitted, have no sense or beauty in combination, and can only become intelligible when the pianoforte is added. They must be perfect in themselves, and in relation to each other, without any assistance from it. The quality of their tone is so far removed from that of the piano that, whenever they are playing, their individual parts will be markedly prominent in all their aspects. If they do not combine well melodically, the faulty workmanship will be startlingly evident. The two trios of Beethoven, Op. 70, No. 1 in D and No. 2 in E flat (more especially the latter) are the best possible object lessons in this treatment. The first four bars of the first allegro of the E flat trio are an admirable example in themselves — the main figure of the first four notes in octaves, followed by two parts of great beauty, sounding quite satisfactory even alone, enriched by a third part on the pianoforte as melodious as they are, but not essential to the grasping of the phrase:

Throughout the trio the strings alternately talk to each other and combine as would two singers in an opera, always having something interesting to say, and, when they have not, saying nothing at all, but wisely trusting to those great antidotes of monotony, rests.

In quartets and quintets for pianoforte and strings the same principles apply; the basis of writing being four-part and five-part respectively. The family of strings when they are combined must always be given music which is complete in itself, and independent of, though dovetailing into, the pianoforte. The models for all these combinations are in plenty — the trios of Mozart, Beethoven, Schubert, Brahms; the quartets and quintets of the same composers, and of Schumann and Dvořák; and for the combination of pianoforte and wind instruments (which follow exactly the same lines) the works of Mozart (clarinet trio and quintet for pianoforte and wind), Beethoven (trio for pianoforte, clarinet and 'cello, quintet for pianoforte and wind, sonata for pianoforte and horn, etc.), Schumann (pieces for pianoforte and oboe, and pianoforte and clarinet), Brahms (trio for pianoforte, violin and horn, sonatas for pianoforte and clarinet), Saint Saëns (caprice for pianoforte, flute, oboe and clarinet, a most interesting study even from the purely technical point of view apart from its musical charm), and a host of other works great and small.

The bearing of colour upon the treatment of voices, alone and in combination with instruments, requires a chapter to itself.

The secret of obtaining mastery of tints and of mixing colours well is only gained by a wide knowledge of musical works, and by using every opportunity of hearing them. The composer must be as well equipped in his literature as the poet or the philosopher. He will not preserve his freshness unless he keeps his ears open and his brains alive to all that is going on round him. The inventions of others will often strike sparks out of himself, will broaden his sympathies and widen his horizon. The two greatest historical examples of eternal freshness and youth in musical history are Haydn and Verdi. They were never too proud to learn from their contemporaries, or even from those far junior to themselves, and they are a standing and ever-living proof that the absorption of all that is best in other men's work only means to the man of genuine invention the accentuation of his own individuality.

CHAPTER VIII

THE TREATMENT OF VOICES

THE first tendency of a student when dealing with the human voice is to forget that it is not an instrument upon which the notes can be obtained by striking on a key or pressing on a string. The singer has to make his own notes; he has to start singing from a point which is intelligible to his ear, and to make his intervals from his inner perception. When those intervals are difficult, the road to them must be made smooth, and the difficulty must not be enhanced by their surroundings. All the skips which are forbidden in strict counterpoint are naturally difficult for the voice; not, perhaps, so much so to an ear accustomed to the modern developments of music as they were when the rules of counterpoint were made (in the interest of singers), but even now requiring a very accurate ear to preserve pure intonation when they are attempted. Every chorus-master knows the danger which besets his forces when they have to sing even so apparently straightforward a succession of notes as . The B will always have a tendency to be too flat; the ear will rightly make the C close to the B; the octave, therefore, will be arrived at below the pitch, and the whole body of singers will flatten. In the sixteenth century the skip of the major sixth was not permissible. The underlying reason for that rule is still apparent from the example given above. The addition of instrumental accompaniment to the voice has enlarged its possibilities in attacking difficult intervals, owing to the suggestion of chords and modulations which it gives; but the inclination often is to presume too far upon the voice and to trust to the instrument for helping it over the stiles, with the result that the part becomes ungrateful to the singer and what is usually termed "unvocal." The interest is speedily transferred to the instrument, and the singer is made to play a secondary rôle in the combination. The human voice is not adapted for hops, skips and jumps, except where declamation peremptorily demands them. Their abuse inevitably leads to such a deterioration of the organ as no wise artist will face. He will not forego his chances of making a livelihood to please any composer, and quite rightly does not care to sacrifice poetry of motion to dangerous gymnastics. The student must always keep in mind the practical fact that ungrateful music for the voice is always ineffective in its appeal to the listener.

We will first consider vocal music from the standpoint of the song, with pianoforte accompaniment. Whole stacks of songs are written and published which are of no practical use for performance whatever. They are paper songs, which may be even musically interesting, but which, from the unpractical manner in which they are written, are obviously unsuited for performance and unattractive to the singer. This is one of the many reasons why the writing of a good

THE TREATMENT OF VOICES

song is one of the most difficult tasks which a composer can undertake. Another reason is that a song is a miniature and has to be so perfect in every detail that it will bear examination under a magnifying glass. Another is that it has to express in the most compressed and yet intelligible form emotions, which at first sight seem too great for the limited boundaries within which it must perforce be confined. Another is that the poetry to which it is set is (or should be) the chief consideration, and that the music should be co-ordinate or subordinate to it without ever being *super*-ordinate. The first step in song writing, therefore, is to grasp the rhythm and the principles of poetry; to study its declamation, through the knowledge not not merely of the prosody, but of the fundamental difference between quantity and accent. A well-known stanza from Shakespeare will illustrate this point, which marked in quantity reads thus:

Full fathom five thy father lies;
Of his bones are coral made;
Those are pearls that were his eyes;
Nothing of him that doth fade,
But doth suffer a sea-change
Into something rich and strange.

and marked in accent thus:

Full fathom five thy father lies;
Of his bones are coral made;
Those are pearls that were his eyes;
Nothing of him that doth fade,

But doth suffer a séa-chánge
Into something rích and stránge.

Adding note-values to each syllable the accurate declamation would be as follows:

Such absolute accuracy of declamation as this it is, of course, impossible to carry out in a measured song. But it can be nearly approached both by the natural accents in each bar, and by the intelligence with which a good singer will insensibly vary the length or shortness of a note in order to bring the music into line with the poem. In addition to this, music is capable of subaccents, owing to the variety of the note-values, by which a singer can bring out the lilt of a verse with even more clearness than a reader can; and words which cannot be prolonged in elocution can be held out on a long note in singing. An intelligible example of this can be given by setting the verse above to note-values, in time and barred.

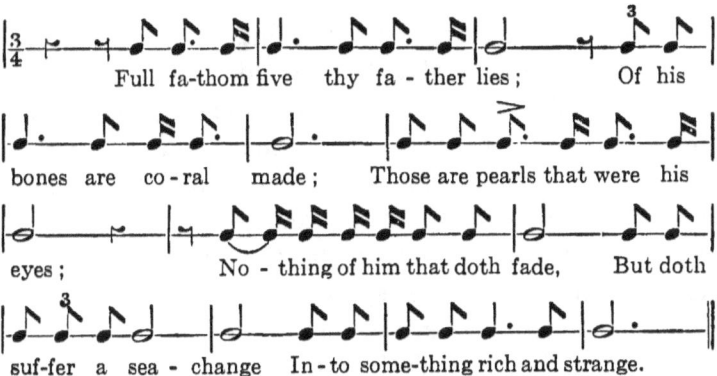

Purcell's setting of this stanza (with the exception of his lengthening of the first syllables of "coral" and "nothing") almost exactly carries out this rough scheme, and shows how it can be as easily reproduced in square time as in ¾:

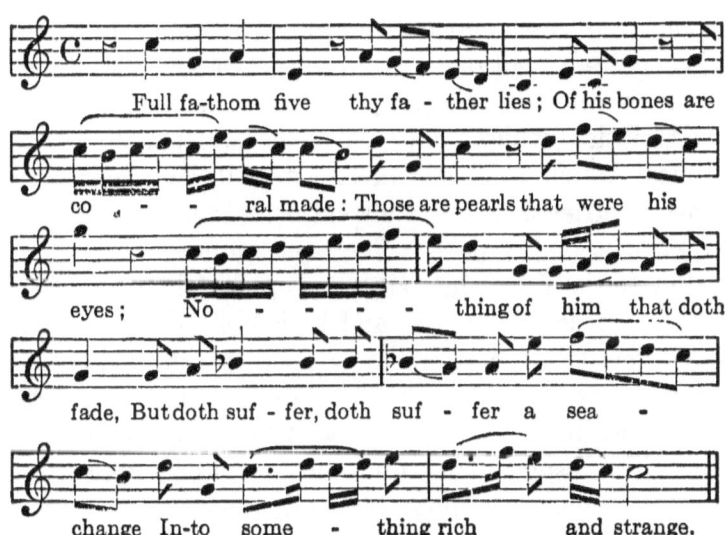

In the words "córăl" and "nóthĭng" Purcell has followed the accent as strongly as the quantity, and has evidently intended "nōthĭng" to balance the long quantity and accent of "sōmethĭng" in the last line. It is worth noticing that there is not one single phrase in the whole of this wonderful melody (even in the modulation in the fifth line) which does not amply explain itself to the ear without help from any accompaniment or harmonisation; and that the composer has contrived to emphasise the close relation between the second and third lines, and to space out the fourth line, by a slight break and rest before it.

The next factor in declamation is to define in music the natural inflections of the poem. The reciter varies his pitch only, the song extends the compass of the reciter and gives an intelligible series of notes where he can only roughly indicate their high or low position. The composer translates this defined rise and fall into melody; but his melody should be conceived so as to coincide with the natural run of the words. He would give more attention to this all-important feature of song writing, if he fully appreciated the limitless possibilities which music has of accentuating the appeal which a poem makes, and if he understood how irretrievably its maltreatment can destroy the intentions of the poet. The poet cannot indicate the pitch or the lilt of his poem, except by the suggestion of the words themselves, and he is obliged to leave all such details, no matter how vital they are to the true rendering of his verse, to the intelligence of the man who reads it. The composer who sets it has, therefore, the great responsibility upon him of interpreting it on the lines which the poet felt, and was unable to write

THE TREATMENT OF VOICES 133

down with the accuracy which is at the musician's command. For an instance of this, the following lines set by Handel in *Samson* will be valuable:

> Total eclipse! No sun, no moon!
> All dark amidst the blaze of noon!

In accent they run thus:

> Tótal eclipse! No sún, no móon!
> All dárk amidst the bláze of noón!

The natural rise (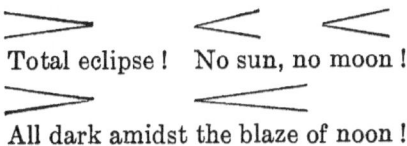) and fall (>) runs thus:

The close accuracy with which Handel has reproduced this in musical setting is a lesson in itself:

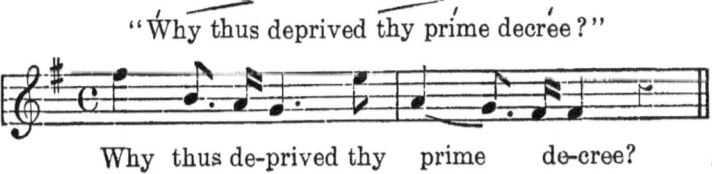

To - tal eclipse! No sun, no moon! All dark a-midst the blaze of noon!

The succeeding lines are no less strikingly reproduced:

> "Why thus deprived thy príme decrée?"

Why thus de-prived thy prime de-cree?

(The accent of "príme decrée" is obtained by position on the strong beat, and length of note.)

(high ———————— >

"Sún, móon and stárs are dárk to me."

Sun, moon and stars   are   dark   to   me.

Any composer, who studies and follows the principles of settings such as this, will not lay himself open to the criticism of poets or to the complaint once expressed by Lord Tennyson to the writer that "so many composers made the notes go up when he wanted them to go down, and go down when he wanted them to go up"; and he instanced, with something approaching indignation, Balfe's setting of "Come into the garden, Maud," which, instead of giving the rise,

"Come into the gárden, Maud,"

gave a fall,

"Cóme into the garden, Maud,"

and utterly destroyed his line and the accentuation of it.

Another vital consideration which must be rigidly remembered in song writing is that the world of singers is divided into sopranos, mezzo-sopranos, contraltos, tenors, baritones and basses, and the vocal part must be written for the compass of any one of these, but not for an admixture of any two of them, a very common fault of the inexperienced beginner. Moreover, each of these voices has a certain range of notes, equidistant from the extremes of its compass, within which

THE TREATMENT OF VOICES

the main part of his vocal notes must lie. This is called the "Tessitura" of the voice.

It is easier for a singer to reach extreme notes if he is not previously fatigued by the strain of a series of passages which are above or below the tessitura. The method of writing vocal music in the clefs formerly

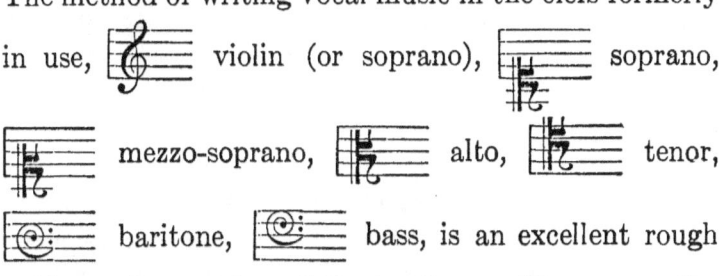

in use, violin (or soprano), soprano, mezzo-soprano, alto, tenor, baritone, bass, is an excellent rough guide to the position of the tessitura. The nearer the average of notes keeps to the middle line of the five, and the closer the vocal part revolves round that as a centre, the better is the tessitura of the song. Ledger lines above and below represent the extremes of compass which are to be used more exceptionally and for special effects.

This rule is just as important to the writer of songs as the compass of orchestral instruments is to the writer of symphonies. No song which does not conform to it is of any practical use except to the collector of curiosities. The avoidance of writing high notes to difficult vowels (such as "o") is, with other requirements of the voice, best studied by consulting a singer or a singing master, a precaution too often neglected by the young composers who are most careful to take expert advice upon instrumental limitations.

The accompaniment of a song should be only a comment on its meaning. It should be suggestive of its colour and atmosphere without being obtrusive. Its elaboration should be as an undercurrent, and should be felt rather than heard. Its simplicity should never give an idea of being studied. The moment an accompaniment distracts the attention from the poem and the singer, it is overstepping the line and spoiling the balance. When an intervening passage for the pianoforte alone occurs, it should never be so long as to interrupt the run of the poem or to break its continuity of idea. For this reason a break in the middle of a verse should generally be very short, while one between the verses can usually be longer. Both are valuable, for the sake of the song as well as of the singer; but the necessary breathing space and rest which it gives to the voice must coincide with common sense and with the exigencies of the poem, and must never be so accentuated as to call undue attention to itself.

It may be safely said, that there is no song of Schubert (perhaps the greatest master of that art who ever lived) in which these principles are not carried out. There are no more suggestive and vividly illustrative accompaniments than his, but they are never more than suggestive or illustrative; and they always bear the same relation to the melody and to the poetry that even the very best illustrations do to the text of a well-written book.

The following songs of Schubert will repay the closest study:

The Erl-King. The accompaniment suggests only the storm and the galloping horse.

Gretchen am Spinnrade. The spinning-wheel and its momentary cessation (a marvellously dramatic touch).

THE TREATMENT OF VOICES

Meeres-Stille. The quiet pulse of a calm sea.
Der Doppel-gänger. The mystery of the ghost.
Die junge Nonne. The storm and the nunnery bell.
Abschied. The trotting of the horse.

Any number of these songs can be analysed upon the same method, by following the whole trend and meaning of the poem, ascertaining its central idea, and looking for its illustration in the accompaniment. Whenever the poem is descriptive and requires what is known in theatres as an "elaborate set," the accompaniment is more intensified (as in the "Erl-King"); when the poem is introspective, and appeals more to the soul than to the senses, the accompaniment retires more into the background (as in "An die Musik"). The texture of the pianoforte figures furnishes the means of obtaining this end. Rhythmical figure is the secret of it, and the persistence of such a figure in its varied guises, permutations and commutations gives the subtle quality known as "atmosphere" to the whole. Through all song writing the student must keep in mind that the two chief musical necessities are primarily the melody and secondarily the bass.

Brahms' invariable method, to which we have already alluded, of testing the value of a song by placing his hand over the right-hand part of the pianoforte, and judging it first by the voice part and the bass, is perfectly sound. If either of them fail to interest, the song will be fundamentally poor; no amount of good texture in the accompaniment will save it, any more than good colouring will give life to a badly-drawn picture.

There is also a type of song in which the "atmosphere" is given by the voice and the illustration by the accompaniment. Certain suggestions of pictorial poetry such as the call of a bird or the running of a stream cannot be expressed by the part allotted to the voice without becoming grotesque. For these the composer must rely on the pianoforte, and the singer must give the colour. Of this type of song the "Leiermann" of Schubert is an instructive instance. The voice part is in itself almost monotonous and purely subjective. The piano reproduces the drone of the hurdy-gurdy and its almost inconsequent melody. The singer, as it were, stands at the street corner, listens to the itinerant player and comments upon him. Schubert gives the singer all the atmosphere and the pianoforte all the illustration of the scene. But as songs of this type must in their nature become tiresome if they are too spun out they must always be short. Economy of material is of the highest value here. The fewer the notes (provided that there are enough of them to express the meaning intelligibly), the better the song. Its success depends upon the power known as suggestion, and the means used ought, therefore, to be rather suggestive than elaborate.

It is well to avoid writing several notes to one syllable except when the melody demands them, or when they are made a special feature of rhythmical detail. Archbishop Cranmer's maxim not to put two notes to a syllable when one will do is a safe one to follow. In the days of *coloratura* singing the custom was different, but a glance at the operas of Rossini will show that such gymnastics were confined to the settings of words which were of little or no importance to the dramatic action, and that where incisiveness of declamation was necessary, recitative only was employed.

THE TREATMENT OF VOICES 139

Such "stage-waits" are now minimised, and brilliant passages for the voice have had to yield to dramatic and poetic necessity. What is true of opera applies still more to songs, where all the sense and trend of the poem is condensed into a small space.

Songs can also be divided into two general types, those which are in verse form, and those which are in one extended form termed by the Germans "durchcomponirt."

(1) *Songs in verse form.* The simplest examples of this (the most common) type are folk-songs. One vocal melody is made to do service for every stanza without change. The adoption of this form must entirely depend upon the poem which the composer chooses for setting. Some poems lend themselves with ease to this treatment; others require many alterations in the successive verses in order to suit changed accents and differing positions of the breaks in the sentences. In the following lines from the first and second verses of a lyric by Henley, this difficulty will become obvious:

    Verse 1. 1. The spring, my dear,
                 2. Is no longer spring.
                 3. Does the blackbird sing
                 4. As he sung last year?

    Verse 2. 1. Though life be change,
                 2. It is hard to bear
                 3. When the old sweet air
                 4. Sounds forced and strange.

The first verse requires a definite break between lines 2 and 3. The second verse is broken after line 1, and lines 2, 3 and 4 must run in one continuous flow. It is not possible, or scarcely possible, to find a melody which will fit both without modification. Hymnology is rich in these alterations of accent and break, and the Procrustean methods of making all the verses fit somehow into the mechanical repetition of an identical tune lead only too often to the most barbaric absurdities. But in hymns the fault lies with the poet or poetaster, who ought to design his verses in such a way as to assimilate the run of each line to its prototype. In songs the fault would lie with the composer, if he did not alter his melody both in rhythm and design to suit the alterations in the poetry. This form of song, therefore, must be of the nature of an air and variations, in which the singing part varies by rhythm and accent, and the pianoforte part by detail; the amount of variation necessary being decided by the requirements of the words. Schubert provides plenty of examples of this, e.g. "Ungeduld," "Das Wandern," "An die Musik," all unaltered, "Wohin?" altered, and countless others which the student had better investigate and classify for himself.

(2) *Songs in extended form* (= durchcomponirt). These are mostly of the more dramatic type, the poem demanding a continuous and gradually developed illustration. The words are set line by line, rather than verse by verse; the breaks between the stanzas are minimised, and depend upon the run of the story, rather than upon the stereotyped divisions of the printer. Examples: "Der Erl-König," "Ganymed," "An Schwager Kronos," with countless others, *q.v.*

It is in this order of song that the composer is most likely to fall into the trap of instrumental overelaboration. He will escape it, if he always keeps in mind that the poetry is the means whereby the song

THE TREATMENT OF VOICES 141

is made intelligible to the hearer; and that if, even for one moment, he obliterates a sentence of it by overloading his instrumentation, the sense is lost, the thread breaks, and his illustration is automatically deprived of the only possible clue to its meaning. It is as though a woodcut in a book were printed over, instead of opposite to, the text to which it refers. He must not trust to the words being printed in the programme. They should be so printed, but not as excuses for the composer's concealment of them, or for the singer's faulty declamation or enunciation. They are only to enable a listener to see the gist of the whole poem which is to be sung, and to follow with ease the various moods which it interprets.

The best practice in the art of writing accompaniments to both these types is to arrange folk-songs. The colour and sense of every verse must be grasped, and any advisable variations both of harmonies and of figures must conform to them; and as in setting them simplicity is the main consideration, and complexity is only tolerable when it is peremptorily called for by the poetry, the principle of economy of material will be more thoroughly driven home.

But there is, on the other hand, no need to be irritatingly antiquarian in dealing with folk-songs. An arranger need no more follow the sixteenth or seventeenth century than the eighteenth or nineteenth in his formulas. The musician of early times set them in the spirit of his own day, as best suited it, and most easily appealed to his contemporaries. A latter-day composer can express the spirit of his own time without spoiling the flavour of his theme. The melodies of such songs are for all time, their settings must vary with the fashions of a fraction of time. To dress them up in mock antique garments can only make them conspicuous and bizarre. To carry this argument a step further, the melodies of many folk-songs are inherently of the very strongest, and demand proportionately strong treatment if due balance is to be preserved. There is no object in neglecting the results of the advance which music has made from the experience of centuries, when the utilisation of it will enhance their inherent qualities. A composer of the sixteenth century would not have used the style of Dunstable for such purposes; nor would Stevenson, with his Haydnesque proclivities, serve as a pattern for an arranger of Irish melodies now. There is only one golden rule: set them as you feel them, without straining after effects or lopping off modern formulas, if you feel they are natural and appropriate.

In all songs carry out the same principle alluded to in a former chapter on writing for the pianoforte in combination with the violin. The voice, like the violin, is (or should be) trained upon the pure scale. Avoid, therefore, making the accompaniment play the same successive notes in unison with the voice. It is not wanted in that capacity if the singer knows his notes and his intervals, and to double the melody is to fog it. The accompaniment is a distinct part in itself, and to mix it up with the vocal part means loss of power and range to itself. The singer needs all the support he can get in order to be able to be independent in his own sphere, but he does not want his steps to be dogged at every turn, or his imperceptible *rubatos* to be mechanically defined as he makes them. No amount of joint rehearsal will ensure perfect combina-

THE TREATMENT OF VOICES   143

tion under such conditions, for no great artist ever sings a phrase twice alike. It varies with his mood, and with the size of room. The accompaniment, therefore, must allow for elasticity.

Lastly, before setting a poem read it all, and read it aloud, unless you are sufficiently master of the ways and means of poetry to be able to hear its declamation with the help of your eye alone. Many an obscure line will become clarified by this process, and the varying of pace, the rise and fall of the individual sentences, the moments for climax and for rest will all impress themselves on the mind before the musical design is approached.

A piece of advice, which indeed applies to all musical composition, but in a special degree to song writing, may be found useful. If you are gravelled by a difficulty, and it seems, for the time at all events, to be insurmountable, put the whole composition away and let your brain work it out by itself. The brain is an admirable cook, a "cordon bleu," who boils and bakes and fries ideas far away from you in a distant kitchen. He does not ask you to be present while he is at work; if you wait patiently the dish will be quite ready at the right time. "Unconscious cerebration" is the scientific term for this most beneficent property of humanity. A well-ordered brain never forgets. It will take an idea, and improve and refine it out of all knowledge; and it will, if you are in a difficulty, help you out if you do not worry it or yourself. Of the truth of this power the writer may perhaps give an instance from his own experience.

When he was fourteen years old he tried to set a somewhat long dramatic poem as a song. He wrote the first three verses easily enough, but when the drama began to become vivid and to require more power of illustration and design than he possessed, he could not progress an inch, and after several miserable attempts he put it away, and forgot all about it. Ten or eleven years later, when he had quite forgotten his early efforts, he opened a book at the same poem, sat down and wrote it straight off without a hitch. But the surprising proof of "unconscious cerebration" came when, fourteen years after the song was written and published, he found the juvenile attempts in an old box, and the first three verses were both in melody and in harmony, practically identical with those of the completed song. His brain had remembered what he himself had wholly forgotten, and found the way out of the difficulty for him without his being in the least conscious of the process.

Such difficulties frequently arise from the run of a poem, or from some emotional suggestion in its course, for which the musical counterpart does not suggest itself with any spontaneity or ease. This is the way to deal with them. Do not tie your brains into knots in endeavouring to find the way out. Wait until the fog clears of itself and the path is plain.

(3) *Recitative and Arioso.* The practice of writing recitative is most valuable to the song writer, for in it the declamation must be perfect and exactly fitted to the natural inflexions of the words sung. As melodic considerations do not enter into it, except in a very modified degree, the composer can give free play to his dramatic sense, and entirely subordinate his notes to the demands of the words he

THE TREATMENT OF VOICES 145

is setting without being hampered by rhythm of design. The greatest study of recitative which exists is to be found in the *St. Matthew Passion* of Bach, which is an exact reproduction in musical terms of the natural reading by the speaking voice. When it would rise, the music rises; when it would fall, it falls. Even in the setting of the English version, which is a close reproduction of the original German text as set by Bach, the following phrase will show the perfection of his workmanship:

The main difficulty in writing this type of recitative is to bring the sentences within the boundaries of bars and bar-lines without producing any sense of restriction, and to place the important syllables which require the strongest accentuation on the strong beats of the bar itself. If this is carefully thought out, the natural accents will be helped rather than hindered by the barring. The accompaniment should be of the slightest, just sufficient to indicate the

L

direction of the modulations and no more. Any use of themes, or allusions to them, should be between the sentences. There are two accepted forms of recitative proper, dry (*secco*) recitative, and accompanied recitative. In the former there is practically no accompaniment except an occasional chord, and the operas of Mozart supply abundant examples. In the latter the instrumental treatment is much more free, and the vocal part, while preserving its declamatory character, is more fully supported at intervals by the instruments.

Examples of this form are "In quali eccessi" from *Don Giovanni* (one of the finest specimens in existence), "Ah perfido" and "Abscheulicher" (*Fidelio*) of Beethoven. It is sometimes termed "Scena," and as such will be found in many operas.

The arioso is a step nearer the song than the accompanied recitative. It is in many ways more difficult to write than the latter, for it requires a vocal part, which, without definitely departing from recitative style, yet touches on the melodic as well, and an instrumental part which is founded upon rhythm of figure. Bach, again, furnishes the greatest number of fine examples of arioso form, and Gluck was a master of its methods. It is from the arioso and its nearly allied sister, accompanied recitative, that the modern form of opera springs. The entry of Pogner in the first act of the *Meistersinger* is prolonged arioso, pure and simple; quasi-recitative in the voice, rhythmical figure in the orchestra. The relationship between arioso and song is so close that many examples of each can be found which are difficult to define under either name, *e.g.* "In questa, Tomba"

THE TREATMENT OF VOICES

of Beethoven, and "Tod und das Mädchen" of Schubert.

(4) *Unaccompanied Choral Writing.* The purest and finest examples of vocal part-writing are to be found in Palestrina and the Roman school. They are at once the most grateful to sing and the most effective to listen to. The Venetian, Neapolitan and Spanish schools are less perfect, and the Dutch and English are rougher and more experimental.

Complete command of the technique of modal counterpoint is the first necessity in writing for unaccompanied voices. The limitations imposed being set down in the interest of the singers only, practice within those limitations will lay the foundation of grateful vocal writing in a way which no other method can approach. The chief considerations are (1) to start every vocal phrase on a note for which the other parts have prepared the way, and which can be attacked without difficulty; (2) to avoid intervals which are difficult to sing in tune.

Palestrina allowed no skips between the minor sixth and the octave, and forbade all diminished and augmented intervals such as

(The importance of knowing the pure scale will be evident here, for in equal temperament (α) is a minor third, and (β) is a major third.)

Modern developments have made the ear able to master even more difficult intervals than these, but as long as the human voice exists it will find the same difficulty in producing them satisfactorily as it found in the sixteenth century; for mechanical improvements have not as yet found their way into the throat.

When intervals of great difficulty are written, the singer cannot help thinking more of the task of surmounting them than of the words and phrases he is singing, and expression and poetry have to take a second place. The writer more than once has heard a performance at the same concert of a modal madrigal and a complex modern part-song, where the former ended exactly on the pitch and the part-song nearly a tone below it. The fault was with the composer of the part-song, not with the singers. There are plenty of passages of a novelty striking even at the present day to be found even in the works of Palestrina; but if the individual parts are scrutinised, they will always prove to be singable and unstrained. Here is an example of a superb passage in his Mass "O admirabile commercium."

THE TREATMENT OF VOICES 149

(This would be sung at least a tone lower than it is written, the pitch of such music not being, as now, absolute, but modified according to conditions of place, mode and singers' capabilities.) The only difficult entry in this passage is the bass F in the fifth bar, but there are two steps over the stile; the fact that it leaves off in the second bar on G (the next note above F), which is reiterated in the second tenor, and the suggestion given by the B flat in the first tenor immediately before. The modulation to the unexpected minor chord of G, and the equally surprising entry of the chord of F immediately after is attained without a single effort on the part of the individual singers. Another lesson is to be learned from these few bars, which is all-important to the composer of choral works. When force is wanted, the upper registers of the voice should be employed;

when softness is wanted, the lower registers. Of this method Handel is the most instructive master, and *Israel in Egypt* supplies the best examples. The words in the Palestrina excerpt given above, demand an increase of force on "altissimus" and a decrease of "Jesu Christe." This is attained as fully as possible by the high position of the sopranos and tenors, and by the sinking of those voices and the entry of the basses in the last two bars. Compare also "He sent a thick darkness" and the "Hailstone" Chorus from Israel. Sebastian Bach was less compromising and far more experimental in his writing for choral bodies; but even in his most complex movements he never writes an entry so difficult that the ear cannot be guided by the passages which precede it.

The famous shout of "Barabbas" in the *Matthew Passion* looks on paper appalling enough,

but when the chords of the recitative which leads to it are clearly heard,

all hesitation vanishes. What Bach has accomplished

here with the help of the instrumental accompaniment, must be done with the help of the accompanying voices in *a capella* writing.

Difficult intervals involved by modulation can often be avoided by judicious crossing of the parts. For instance, in this passage

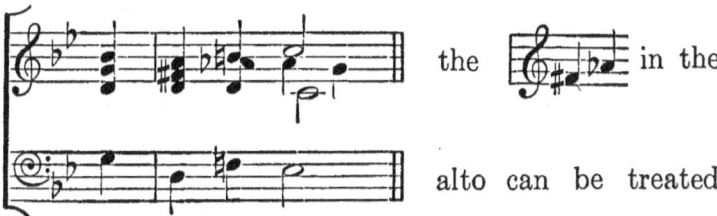

and the student should carefully balance all such progressions, and lay them out in the most easy and vocal manner possible, while preserving the modulations which are necessary to his conception.

thus:

The following examples from the first part of the

152   MUSICAL COMPOSITION

St. Matthew Passion will suffice to show how Bach tackled such a difficulty:

and

In this last example the A flat (which would have presented great difficulties to the altos) is given to the tenors, who take it quite easily from C. In these, as in many other places, the effectiveness of the

THE TREATMENT OF VOICES

declamation gains by crossing the parts, and the contrivance serves the double purpose of greater ease for the singer and clearer incisiveness for the words.

Lastly, give the singers time to breathe. Long series of notes without a break will inevitably result in artificially broken rhythms and unsteady tempi. There is no bellows-blower for a singer's lungs. He must fill them himself, and the composer must provide stopping places where he can carry out that operation without interfering with the run of the music. If he does not do so, the singers will perforce find them for themselves, and will not scruple to break a phrase, or even a word, to do it, perhaps exactly at the spot where it is most ruinous to the composer's meaning. If he intends the break to be taken between two notes, it is better to write

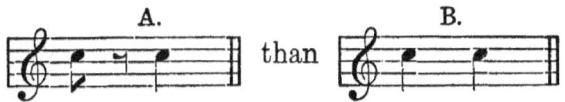

especially in a quick movement. The quaver rest will be there in any case if the singer breathes, and to write it at A, instead of trusting to chance as at B, is the safer policy if good phrasing is to be preserved. What the composer too frequently forgets in many branches of his craft is, that performers do not immediately and intuitively know things which seem self-evident to him, and that he has to legislate very clearly and definitely for the most ignorant and the least experienced. When he means *legato* or *staccato*, he must say so. When he wants a hurrying or slackening of pace, he must put it down. When he writes for voices, he must indicate the phrasing as he would bow or slur his violins. He must remember that if his music is good it will be often performed when he is not present to rehearse, and that an omitted mark or an insufficient suggestion of pace may give an entirely wrong impression of his work. Solo-singing parts can often be overmarked, it is true; because any intelligent vocalist will prefer to give his own reading of a composition in the way which appeals to him most, and no two singers are exactly alike in temperament. To tie him down too much is to the detriment of the rendering he will give, and a great work will bear having various lights thrown upon it by the individuality of the performer. But with masses of voices, as with masses of instruments, it is different; and too great care cannot be bestowed upon writing down clearly and unmistakeably the instructions of the inventor for the guidance of the conductor and the performers alike. The trouble will be amply repaid by the minimising of misery to the composer when he hears his own creations produced before the public.

CHAPTER IX

EXTRANEOUS INFLUENCES IN INSTRUMENTAL MUSIC

Music may be divided into two classes — absolute music, when the art speaks for itself by sound alone, and descriptive music, when it illustrates words or drama. There has always been a tendency, which in recent times has grown into a cult, to allow the second class to trespass upon the first. This type is necessarily a hybrid, but it has grown to such proportions that it requires the fullest consideration in any treatise dealing with composition. There can be no question that music which speaks for itself is not only the purest, but also the most all-embracing form of the art. Being intangible and indefinable, it suggests to different minds different trains of thought, and any defined programme of a movement given by one listener may be miles apart from one given by another. For example, Grove's picturesque conception of the finale of Schubert's Symphony in C, as an illustration of the ride of Phaëthon, may be entirely antipathetic to a listener of different mood and temperament. To abolish this indefinable element in music is to detract from its universal appeal, and to impose limitations upon what is inherently illimitable. Tennyson's brilliant dictum that "Poetry is like shot-silk with many glancing colours; every reader must find his own interpretation according to his ability, and according to his sympathy with the poet," applies in every particular to music also. That certain impressions and certain poems or dramatic ideas do actually suggest musical ideas and forms to a composer is undoubted; but so much vaster is the art with which he deals than any part which he has in it himself, that his own ideas may develop thousands of others in the minds of those who listen to his work. This is the secret of the truth of Beethoven's axiom that, though he always worked to a picture, he never said what that picture was. He did tell once or twice, but never with success. The "Rondo on the Lost Penny" was a joke, the "Battle of Vittoria" was a failure. His most realistic picture was the Pastoral Symphony; but he was careful to stereotype its underlying principle on the front page, and to warn the hearer that it was only "an expression of impressions." Although that work has been often quoted as the parent of modern programme-music, it is nothing whatever of the kind. Its atmosphere is unmistakeable, even if it had never been christened "Pastorale," or its movements labelled with the central idea of each picture they represent. It applies to any country, any landscape, any river, any storm, any merry-making — in a word, it is universal in its appeal; while more recent picture-works rely upon a would-be exact definition of person, place and action. The forefathers of the present programme-music are not the classical masters such as Haydn and Beethoven, but such now-forgotten scribes as Steibelt (Admiral Duncan's Victory), Kotzwara (The Battle of Prague),

INFLUENCES IN INSTRUMENTAL MUSIC 157

and, *mirabile dictu*, Dussek (The Sufferings of the Queen of France). From this somewhat obscure stock descended the first notable men who sowed in this debateable ground, Berlioz and Liszt. Realism was the ground principle of it, and as realism advanced, idealism retreated. Sundry composers of the highest idealistic aims occasionally played with the fascinating siren, such as Spohr, Mendelssohn, Schumann, Sterndale Bennett, but they none of them allowed realism to do more than peep in on rare occasions. If the braying of the ass is reproduced in Mendelssohn's *Midsummer Night's Dream* overture, it must not be forgotten that the work was written for the theatre, where the acting of the play would explain it. The concert-overtures of the same composer are labelled with the names of the persons and things which suggested them, but they are the very reverse of realistic, and would be equally satisfying as pure music without any title at all. The attractiveness of writing programme-music, such as symphonic poems and the like, lies in the comparative freedom from set form and difficult development of ideas which it holds out to the beginner. It is easier to write than absolute music, just as so-called free counterpoint is easier than strict. It imports the more unshackled type of stage-music into the domain of concert-music. It suggests the broad and easy path of inventing whole series of themes instead of the narrow and laborious path of developing a few. But the beginner who first chooses the easy way will rarely be able to retrace his steps or to face the difficulties of the narrow one. It is only the master of all kinds of form who can make it subservient to his ends; he only can effectively dictate his orders to his subordinates, who is their superior in experience and in knowledge.

Programme-music, then, is the incursion of music proper into the realms of the drama. How far can it carry its invasion without being itself destroyed? Only so far as it is intelligible to the ear, without help from any other organ. There are no words or scenic adjuncts to assist it. It must not rely on a title (which may be torn off) or an analysis in a book of words (which may go out of print) for an explanation of the drift of the drama. It must tell a clear story to any musical listener who does not happen to have seen the name, or to have a shilling to buy a programme. If it succeeds under such conditions, it is a work of art; if it does not, it is a work of artificiality. In a word, it must appeal, after all, as absolute music. In a species of music so prevalent in the present day, it is especially interesting to have the views of a composer whom no one save, perhaps, musical post-impressionists would describe as a Philistine or a Tory, Richard Wagner. In his conversations with Edward Dannreuther the following passages occur which throw a search-light on the question:

"Give me Beethoven's quartets and sonatas for intimate communion, his overtures and symphonies for public performance. *I look for homogeneity of materials,* and *equipoise of means and ends.* . . .

"I went straight from Palestrina to Bach, from Bach to Gluck and Mozart — or if you choose, along the same path backwards. . . . In instrumental music I am a Réactionnaire, a conservative. *I dislike everything that requires a verbal explanation beyond the actual sounds.* For instance, the middle of Berlioz's touching *scène*

INFLUENCES IN INSTRUMENTAL MUSIC

d'amour in his 'Romeo and Juliet' is meant by him to reproduce in musical phrases the lines about the lark and the nightingale in Shakspeare's balcony scene, but it does nothing of the sort — it is not intelligible as music. . . . This so-called Symphonic Dramatique of Berlioz's as it now stands is neither fish nor flesh — strictly speaking it is no symphony at all. There is no unity of matter, no unity of style. . . .

"When occasion offered I could venture to depict strange and even terrible things in music, *because the action rendered such things comprehensible*: but music apart from the drama cannot risk this, for fear of becoming grotesque." And in 1879 he wrote "whenever a composer of instrumental music loses touch of tonality he is lost"; adding an example from his own works, which, he said, was intelligible in the theatre with action and words, but impossible in absolute music.

The writer has quoted these excerpts at length, because they are the appeal of one of the greatest masters of our day to the rising generation to abstain from writing formless, illogical and ill-balanced work for the concert room. Wagner would have been the last to disparage such masterpieces as the Leonora or the Freischütz overtures (which are so far programme-music that they illustrate by anticipation the drama which they introduce) or as his own *Flying Dutchman, Tannhäuser, Lohengrin, Tristan, Meistersinger* and *Parsifal* Preludes. All of these will stand the test of being listened to as instrumental music, and will need no explanation to make them intelligible and enjoyable for their own sakes. It is true that they gain in vividness of suggestion when the opera which they precede is familiar to the listener, but as concert pieces they are entirely satisfying without a title or a story. They represent, therefore, the only type of programme-music which can stand on its own feet in the concert-room; and both form and tonality are necessary ingredients in their composition.

The only gauge of the value of a piece of programme-music is the judgment of a sound musician who hears it without knowing its name or its story. If it stands this test, it will justify its existence. If it does not, no amount of sensationalism or brilliant orchestration will lengthen its short life. The construction of symphonic poems depends upon the power of transforming and developing themes and using them to give unity to what otherwise might be an amorphous mass of sound. But the transformation is not enough without the development. Mere repetition or transposition will not suffice to give interest and to avoid monotony. A perpetual series of different themes will only bewilder and give a sense of diffuseness to the listener. History will show abundant examples of highly-gifted composers, in whom the power of invention has been so great and the power of concentration so small, that they have preferred to save themselves the labour of development by substituting new themes at every turn. In all such cases the tragic sequel has been the same; their music is forgotten, or in process of being forgotten. Superficiality is the disease which kills it. This lack of concentration is the danger which besets the path of the writer of symphonic poems, and it can only be surmounted by the same means which give mastery to other more definite forms of composition, economy of material and the logical evolution of themes. These will be found in the best specimens of modern masters who know their technique, and who have not begun their careers by skimming over difficulties, but by meeting them and overcoming them.

The principles which govern symphonic poems apply also to the incidental music to plays. The latitude is greater, because the composer has the benefit of the certainty that his audience will see the dramatic action which suggests his music. He must not forget, however, that except where he writes an undercurrent accompaniment for a scene where the action is proceeding (of which Mendelssohn's *Midsummer Night's Dream* is a wholly admirable example), he is, as a rule, anticipating action to come, rather than commenting on situations which are past. His overture and entr'actes, therefore, must be intelligible as absolute music, giving the atmosphere of the play rather than relying on realistic moments. The greatest monument in all musical literature of perfect work in this type is Beethoven's music to Goethe's Egmont. It never interferes with the play itself, but it illustrates it at every turn. The stroke of genius which emphasises the arrest of Egmont as the curtain falls, and uses it as a bridge to the entr'acte which succeeds, is one of the most startling dramatic moments in all music. It is unfortunately seldom heard in the theatre, for audiences all over the world, and even in the most musical countries, will applaud when the curtain falls, and talk all through the music, when it has come down and the lights go up; and the average public cannot be expected to know Beethoven's score so well as to make an exception in favour of these immortal ten seconds. The passage, however, is fortunately on

M

paper, and the student can realise its effect with his eye.

Melodrama, as music is termed which is played while the curtain is up, must be so designed as to quarrel as little as possible with the actor's voice. It is best used in the intervals of dialogue, and, when it actually accompanies it, should be kept far distant from the pitch of the speaker. Even when the phrases are short, they should always be suggestive of some link with the musical design of the whole; "leading motives," in fact, on a small and well-defined scale.

The sphere of chamber-music has, until quite recent times, been untouched by the tendencies which have produced quasi-dramatic orchestral compositions in looser form. Latterly, however, experiments have been made in a revival of the old "Fancies" or "Fantasies" of early times. The reason for their existence may not improbably be a natural rebellion against the excessive length (and disproportionate interest) of many modern works. It is not given to every one to have the power to magnetise an audience with themes and workmanship for the same length of time that a Beethoven can; nevertheless, many try to make up in length for what they lack in invention. All abuses lead to revulsion of feeling: the greater the grievance, the more drastic is the remedy. The form which the remedy has taken is to condense all the movements of a work in sonata form into one. Like everything under the sun, this is not new. Schumann did it in the D Minor Symphony, Mendelssohn in the Violin Concerto, but the movements are still there in spite of the links which join them. The "Fantasy"

INFLUENCES IN INSTRUMENTAL MUSIC

has only three courses open to it; either it is a single movement without companions, or it is a series of short movements held together by a chain, or it is what Wagner, in the excerpt quoted above, called "Neither fish nor flesh," in other words, amorphous. The writing of such a work therefore is, from the point of view of concentration, far more difficult than that of the older broken form, and if the balance is not observed to a fraction, it will be invertebrate. The student had better, therefore, note at once that the writing of "Fantasies" is not the broad and easy way out of difficulties that it appears to be at first sight. He must also remember the value of moments of silence in music, those gaps which rest the hearer in the intervals, and by their very rarity attract his attention in the course of the movement. They are the breathing places for the lungs of sound. If a fantasy exceeds the length of a movement in sonata form, the excuse that there are no other movements to follow it will not avail to acquit the composer of the offence of outlasting his welcome. This tabloid preparation of the three or four movements of a sonata must contain all the ingredients of the prescription, and yet not exceed the proportions of any one of them. Then, again, the themes must be clear and intelligible to the hearer, and this needs what is termed "spacing." The difficulty of ensuring this, without loss of breathing room when they are concentrated into the smallest possible space, must be obvious. If they are planted too closely together, it will be impossible to see the wood for the trees. The subjects, therefore, must be conceived in miniature so as to ensure their proportion to each other and to the whole design. A composer cannot set himself a more exacting problem. All such experiments, however, are worth trying, provided that a reference to past history does not show (as it often does) that they have been made before and found wanting. These side-paths of the art are attractive as a relief from the high roads, but they are apt to end in an *impasse* and a retracing of the footsteps. The road may be sometimes dusty and sometimes heavy, but it was made by the experience of our forefathers, who found out the best direction for ensuring our progress. It is the road which enables us to reach the side-paths; and to that road, unless we wish deliberately to be lost in the wilderness, we must return. The track itself may seem monotonous, but it is ever giving us new views of the scenery, and varied outlooks upon the country through which we pass as we tread it.

CHAPTER X

DANGER SIGNALS

In the introductory chapter of this little treatise we laid stress on the fact that its main functions must necessarily be to give hints as to what to avoid. Constructive advice in musical composition is practically confined to technique, and natural invention and inspiration cannot be taught. Criticism is the only means of regulating it, that of a superior in experience when the composer is starting on his career, and of himself when he has felt his feet. The only basis of such criticism is taste, and the ability which it gives of judging between what is good and bad — in other words, what is beautiful and ugly in art. To make self-criticism valuable, the taste must be refined to its purest point, but it must stop short of over-refinement, which, instead of giving polish to music when written, may, from breeding over-conscientiousness, prevent the music being written at all. Some young composers think too little, others too much. The one extreme is as dangerous as the other. Let the imagination run, and criticise it for yourself after it has had its fling. If you cannot at once look on your creations with a sufficiently impartial eye, put them away until you have given them time to be partially forgotten. One of the greatest of modern symphonies was in its composer's desk for ten years before he even had the band parts copied. It sounds to this day as spontaneous as if it had been written in as many days.

It is the function of this chapter to point out some of the directions in which this self-criticism may be directed, and to warn the young composer of the traps and snares which he has to avoid.

(§ 1) The danger of altering the pace of a movement unconsciously in the mind, when intending to write in the same *tempo*.

This is a most common failing, and sometimes can only be cured drastically by the intervention of the metronome. (It is assumed, of course, that the composer is wise enough to write at his table and not at the piano.) The form of composition which it most of all affects is unaccompanied writing for voices. When a movement begins in $\frac{4}{4}$ time, the notes will unconsciously become shorter in value as it proceeds, and not infrequently become twice as quick, the $\frac{4}{4}$ time becoming $\frac{2}{2}$. Thus the balance of the design is entirely upset, and the whole intention of the movement is destroyed. The change of *tempo* in this form of work is almost always in the direction of acceleration, seldom or never of retardation. The composer will discover it quickly enough when he tries his manuscript on the pianoforte; but it will then be too late to recast it, for the gradual and continuous steps by which the hurrying has progressed will make it impossible to rectify the balance without rewriting. In instrumental movements, such as the first movement of a piece in sonata-form, the tendency is usually the other way; it principally concerns the second subject, which is

DANGER SIGNALS

often insensibly conceived in a slower time than the first. This is equally disturbing to the balance if it goes so far as to make the second subject impossible or ridiculous to listen to at the pace of the first. Any alteration of its *tempo* must be absolutely superficial, and only in the interests of expression and interpretation (like a *ritardando, accelerando, crescendo* or *diminuendo*).

If the change is vital to its existence, it must be ruled out of court. To give an instance: in the first movement of the Pathetic Symphony, Tschaikowsky has marked the second subject in a slower *tempo*; but though it gains in effect at performance by this indication, it is quite possible to play it at the same speed as the opening of the *allegro* without destroying its intention. The gain of the slower time is in the intensifying of its character, not in its alteration. The only cure for this disease is a rigid discipline of the mind to think in well-balanced time. If the metronome is called in as a corrector, it should be used more and more sparingly and at longer intervals, merely to test the rate at which the invention is working. It will soon be discarded when the brain acts as its own speed-gauge.

(§ 2) The danger of using the terms *ritardando* and *accelerando* as an integral part of a passage, to make a rhythm which sounds too short longer, or one which sounds too long shorter.

The rhythms must be perfect in themselves; these indications are only "trimmings" for giving additional expressiveness to them. A passage which halts has something inherently wrong in itself; one which gives an impression of being cut too short to satisfy the ear is equally so. For example, a concluding phrase such as this

will not be given the rhythm it requires by marking a *ritardando* over the last bar. It must be written thus:

To this phrase any alterations of *tempo* can be applied without damaging its proportions, *e.g.*:

or

This applies also to pause-marks, which must be only ornamental additions.

(§ 3) The danger of ending a movement unsatisfactorily from a rhythmical point of view.

This is one of the greatest difficulties which the inexperienced composer has to combat. He will most commonly be content with a finish which is in reality no finish at all, which leaves the movement "in the air," and gives a feeling of uncertainty in the listener as to whether it is over or not. Its equivalent on the

DANGER SIGNALS

stage is the letting down of the curtain too soon or too late, a mechanical process which, as dramatists know, can wreck the success of a play. The uncomfortable pause and silence which the composer may often experience between the close of his work and the tentative beginning of the applause of the audience, he may (if his composition is otherwise appreciated) set down to something rhythmically wrong in his final bars. "When a piece is over, it is over," as an astute stage-manager once said. He might have added that it is no less important that the listeners should be as conscious of the moment of its finish as they are of the moment of its start. A bar too much or too little may do the mischief. Every one concerned, performers and audience alike, must be unanimous as to the precise second when the end should come. It is impossible to give any rule or even advice which will ensure this satisfactory consummation. It depends upon the whole of the coda which precedes it. The nearest approach to a rule-of-thumb would be to end the last chord either on the third bar of a four-bar rhythm or on the bar which follows that rhythm. The first movement of the Eroica Symphony supplies an example of the first:

The following is a specimen of an ending on the bar following the four-bar rhythm:

But the whole question is a matter of experience and of sound musical instinct. The student will learn best how to do it right by many sufferings from doing it wrong.

(§ 4) The danger of using an insufficient number of rests and silences.

They are the most valuable assets of the composer. As has been said in a former chapter, they are the breathing places of music. "Let the air in" was the frequent burden of Hans von Bülow's advice both to players and writers. In all chamber-music they fill a leading rôle. A string quartet will be stodgy and monotonous in the extreme without them. Wind instruments must have them, both to allow time for the player to fill his lungs and to rest his lip. The pianist also needs them to rest his muscles, the audience to rest their ears. It has been truly said that some of the most thrilling moments in music have been the result of a dead silence (cf. the entry of the Dutchman in the second act of Wagner's opera, the silences after "Hear and Answer" in the familiar Baal chorus of the *Elijah*, and, perhaps the most impressive

DANGER SIGNALS

of all, the silence which succeeds the Trumpet Call in the second act of *Fidelio*). To hit upon the right moment for this effect is no easy matter; it must never miss fire, and never sound like a complete finish. To do it successfully requires a dramatic mind; but all composers must be endowed with that gift if their music is to possess any measure of vitality. Another more utilitarian and perhaps less heroic virtue of rests is the help they give in solving a difficult piece of technique. Many are the knots in part-writing which they will untie in far easier fashion than an alteration of notes. A student will often puzzle his brains for hours to find his way out of an apparent *impasse* which the cessation of a part will clear up at once. Rests and pauses are the best friends of the composer, the performer and the listener.

(§ 5) The danger of falling into a style of orchestration which resembles the perpetual use of the full swell of an organ.

This is closely related to the danger alluded to above. Its genesis is an absence of rests. There is no organ effect more impressive than the full swell, but none more conducive to monotony if it is used in excess. Like all luxury, it ends by palling. The possession of a large fortune does not give nearly so much pleasure to a rich man, as an unexpected five-pound note does to a poor one. Much of recent orchestral writing is so persistently lavish of its resources that the individual characteristics of the various instruments are obliterated altogether. Such poetical conversations between them as delight the ear in Schubert's unfinished symphony are ceasing to be. Instead of rivers and brooks of sound winding through a changing scenery of fields and woods, we have nothing but the ocean to look at. This backward step in the use of the finest instrument in the world, the orchestra, cannot be otherwise than a passing phase. It has its uses, both in advancing the technique of instrumental playing, and in helping experiments in the colour of vast combinations. The process is fascinating, especially to a beginner, who takes in it the same somewhat wicked joy that a young organist takes in playing with all his stops out. Later on he comes back to the purer enjoyment of a single diapason. Not so long ago, before the days of hydraulic engines and electricity, the organ blower used to moderate the transports of the too spendthrift organist by letting the wind out, and threatening a strike. That wholesome, if annoying, corrective had its uses, like the metronome; but the player, like the orchestrator, has now to work out his own salvation. As he wakes to the fact that perpetual high pressure of sound does away with all possibilities of climax, he will find relief in the more sympathetic method of alternating and combining single stops. So it is with the conditions prevailing in much modern orchestration. Composers have been naturally magnetised by the richness and sonority which Wagner obtains with his orchestra *at moments of climax*, and have smeared them all over their scores irrespective of balance of colour or design. Every phrase is as highly coloured as its neighbour, and all power of strong contrast disappears. This is the precise reverse of the orchestral theories of the most imaginative and experimental orchestrator of modern times, Berlioz. He knew too well the glories and beauties of individual

DANGER SIGNALS

instruments to encourage his successors to throw them all into a cauldron and boil them up together. If his invention and melodic power had been equal to his poetical command over the orchestra; if, in a word, he had been as great a draughtsman as he was a colourist, his influence would have been paramount at the present day. The combined characteristics of Wagner and Berlioz, the collectiveness of the one and the individualism of the other, if the value of their music had been on an equality, would have kept the orchestral road clear. These luxurious outbursts are too often used to conceal poverty of invention. "The greater the number of staves in the score, the fewer the number of ideas," was an astute comment on the situation by a great conductor. The best antidote to this plethora of material is a solid grounding in writing for a small orchestra, such as sufficed for Mozart, and, in the main, for Beethoven. A composer who can produce such colour as Wagner did in his Siegfried Idyll, with the same limited means, will find it far easier to dispose larger forces when he is called upon to command them, and his experience in controlling smaller bodies will lead gradually up to a greater ability in handling army corps. He will know his units and their capabilities, individual as well as collective, and will not strain them beyond their powers. He will, for example, treat his horn-players as human beings, not as padding to fill up chords, and he will never lose sight of the two most valuable assets of an orchestrator, contrast of colour and economy of material.

(§ 6) The danger of lack of economy in material.
The student must remember that the more

performers he requires for his works, the less likely he is to secure the frequent performance of them.

Operas with a small number of characters, and with the minimum of elaborate scenic effects, have the best chance of acceptance. A symphony which requires many extra instruments has a limited appeal. Bass clarinets, cors anglais, bass trumpets, contra-bass trombones are not grown on every bush, and, quite apart from the expense of engaging them, their presence can only be secured in a small minority of orchestras. A widely popular and well-established master may attract a sufficient audience to warrant the outlay they necessitate, but a lesser-known man (however able) will only be setting up obstacles to his own career by employing them as *necessities*. The arrangement of a movement from a big score for a limited band, say a theatre orchestra of twenty or so, will be both interesting as practice and useful as showing how much can be done by handling a few players effectively. The composer will often be surprised at the very slight modifications of colour which such a procedure will involve; how little the lower notes of an oboe will differ from the medium notes of a cor anglais; how well two bassoons will combine with two horns, and give an effect approximating that of four; how the *cuivré* or brassed sounds of the horns can help out upper trombone parts, and many other such devices. The shades of the colours may not be so minute, but their general tone is not so different as to spoil the drift of the composer's meaning. Routine in this branch of orchestral technique will provide him with many ways of securing alternatives for absent instruments; and the more he uses them, the less torture will he suffer from omitted passages or incomplete harmonies. This is especially true of scores in which an organ has any important part, for it is not every concert hall which possesses one, and even when it does, the instrument may be at an impossible pitch or out of tune. In a word, the composer must cultivate the virtue of practicality, and make it easy for his works to be performed, instead of, like Frankenstein, raising up monsters which will destroy him.

(§ 7) The danger of losing sight of the characteristics of the means used for expressing the ideas.

No music is written indefinitely without any fixed intention as to what medium of sound-production is to perform it, but only too frequently the boundaries between the various instruments are ignored. Strings are given pianoforte passages, brass instruments are given string passages, double basses are treated like organ pedals, the pianoforte like an orchestra. The sooner this muddy mixture of the colour and the capabilities of individual instruments is cleaned out the better. The mind should be clear as to the instrument for which it is designing sounds; it should instinctively hear it while it invents for it. To write for the piano with the organ in the mind would result in passages involving long holding notes, of which it is wholly incapable. To expect the double bass to sustain a long note *forte* as if it were a bass tuba is absurd. Still more common, unfortunately, is the treatment of the human voice as if it were a wind-instrument with keys and an immense compass. Write definitely for given instruments: vocal music for voices, string music for strings, pianoforte music for pianoforte, and do not use the technique suitable for one in writing for another. The foundation for this most necessary discipline can be laid in harmony exercises, which should always be written either for voices or for named instruments. The antique method of putting down notes in them without considering what the quality of their sound would be, or what kind of medium is to produce it, is neither fish, flesh nor fowl. The sooner it is abolished, the better for the student.

(§ 8) The danger of building a large superstructure upon a shallow foundation.

Themes must be proportioned in scope and length to that of the movement which comprises them. The first movement of a symphony demands subjects which are longer and more suggestive than a scherzo or a minuet. Otherwise the intermediate episodes, the development section, and the coda will not have enough material to preserve their interest, and the composer will soon find himself in the unhappy dilemma of trying to make bricks without straw. Similarly, a short movement which has a subject of too large proportions will be clumsy to handle, and will be overweighted at the start. The rules which regulate the construction of plays are equally applicable to musical forms. The five-act tragedy needs ampler material, more gradually developed situations, and a larger basis of interest than a one-act comedy, otherwise the theme will be worn threadbare, and its hold over the spectators will diminish as the play proceeds. The exact balance between the dimensions and details of a musical work can only be hit off by long experience and close acquaintance with accepted masterpieces. We may couple with this

DANGER SIGNALS

(§ 9) The danger of using big means for little ends. The adage of "using a Nasmyth hammer to crack a nut" is a homely method of explaining this snare. Many an intrinsically fine work, especially in opera, has been spoilt by a neglect of its lesson. Overloading of orchestration is a frequent symptom of this weakness. If the student of opera will compare the full scores of *Otello* and *Falstaff*, he will have before him (from the ripe judgment of Verdi) an unsurpassable instance of the subordination of means to ends. The sestet "Sola, sola," in Mozart's *Don Giovanni*, will be equally valuable on a smaller scale, the various movements and situations which it comprises being all treated, both vocally and orchestrally, in exact proportion to their importance in the dramatic situation. So in orchestral work, a delicate symphony like the G minor of Mozart is scored with a lighter hand than the E flat or the C major. The Pastoral Symphony of Beethoven is a kaleidoscope of the most delicate colours; the C Minor Symphony, a massive wall of sound as impenetrable as its theme. Let your clothes fit your figure.

(§ 10) The danger of overloading and over-elaborating less important moments.

Every work, great and small, has its alternations of *arsis* and *thesis*, rise and fall. The instinct which marks down *crescendo* and *diminuendo*, *forte* and *piano*, *accelerando* and *ritardando*, must adapt itself also to the larger field of the structure itself. If every sentence of a speech is at the same level of interest, there will be no great moments of climax. There must be valleys as well as mountains, or the landscape will be a monotonous plain whether its elevation be low or high. Every picture has its points of high light and its tracts of lower colour-values. Every line of poetry has its small and unaccentuated words, unimportant in themselves, but supplying the links between those which arrest the ear. The neglect of this economy of expression induces thickness and stodginess. Every point of interest kills its neighbour. The difficulty lies in filling up the gaps between the important moments with material which is not mere padding, but interesting in itself, and yet not so interesting as to rivet the attention and attract it to the detriment of the outstanding features. Every student of Shakespeare knows the consummate stage-craft with which he opens a play or an act: the first few lines are always so conceived that they contain no important sentence which can be rendered inaudible by the rustle or "settling-down" of the audience. Not that the poetry is careless or useless or padding when read, but the dramatist keeps back his more vital lines for the moments when the interest is prepared for them. On this principle the composer must work, and the longer his design is, the more extended must be these intervals of brain-rest. A parallel once more from the sister art of painting may illustrate this point with still greater clearness. The San Sisto Madonna of Raphael consists of six figures: the Virgin and the Child in the centre, one figure on the left, another on the right, and two cherubs at the foot. These are the outstanding features of the design. The rest of the canvas is what would technically be termed background; a casual glance at it would describe it as sky and clouds A closer investigation will reveal the fact that it is a multitude of cherubs' heads, painted in so shadowy and indefinite a manner that they never attract attention to themselves. This represents the "unimportant moments" of the design. It is not mere blue sky put in as padding, but a poetical design laid out on a lower scale of interest, and painted with lower colour-values than the six outstanding figures. This principle can be as well applied to music as to architecture or to poetry, or indeed to any work of art.

(§ 11) The danger of expressing ideas realistically to one's own mind, without certainty that it will be intelligible as music to the ears of others.

This has been so fully dealt with in the chapter upon extraneous influences in instrumental music that it is scarcely necessary to enlarge upon it here. The composer of programme-music must write it in two capacities, he must be able to criticise his work in the character of an independent listener who does not know his programme, as well as in that of the author who does. Otherwise he will be either obscure or ridiculous, as Dussek was when he described the execution of Marie Antoinette by a descending *glissando* scale on the pianoforte.

(§ 12) The danger of improvising without method.

This is a fascinating amusement, which can have the most dire results. It is the sworn foe of power of construction, and the ally of slipshod workmanship. It aids and abets that most undesirable method of composing, writing at the pianoforte. The instrument should only be used as a test of work done, never (with one exception) as a suggestive medium for the materials of a work. That exception is the technical laying-out of passages intended primarily for the instrument, as a violin player would, if he were a composer, get suggestions from experimenting with passages on the violin.

Nine-tenths of the ideas, no matter how beautiful they may be, which a composer may invent in improvisation, are forgotten as soon as they are played. They are waste of substance, valuable products of the brain, which throws them away as fast as it creates them. To improvise *with method* has a certain value of its own. It needs sense of balance, in order to keep the movement clear in design, and a long and accurate memory to insure the exact repetitions of themes. But it is only a rare genius who can fulfil these conditions without a long previous experience in writing at the table, using his eyes as his ears. No composer of the first rank ever wrote at the pianoforte, or hammered out melodies with his fingers. One who did (not of the first rank) showed the mark it left upon him at every turn. It so affected his belief in his own certainty of touch, that he used to orchestrate passages in different coloured inks in order to be able to choose in rehearsal the form which he preferred. It obliged him to take three flats in his town house, of which he inhabited the middle one, so that no one above or below should hear his music in process of being cooked upon the pianoforte. It so far affected his sense of the effect his dramatic climaxes would produce upon audiences, that he used to sit next the "chef-de-claque" at the Grand Opera at rehearsals, and even take hints from him as to emendations in the passages which suggested applause. Man of genius though he was, as any man who wrote the fourth act of the *Huguenots* must have been, Meyerbeer is a sign-post of this danger of trusting to the pianoforte as a medium for inspiration. The young composer, who is ill-equipped with finger technique, may console himself with the knowledge that Richard Wagner (*teste* Dannreuther) played the pianoforte abominably.

(§ 13) The danger of anticipating the introduction of a key towards which a modulation is in progress.

This is a very common trap for the beginner. It has been described in every-day language as knocking at the door and running away. For instance, the following short modulation from F major to A minor is spoilt by the anticipatory chord of A minor at *:

which can be avoided thus:

This snare is most frequently set in the development section of sonata form, where, unless the modulations are carefully designed, the original key of the movement will appear before its natural place of re-entry, the return of the first subject. The reappearance of the tonic will be robbed of all its freshness if it is heard a moment too soon; the more firmly the tonality has been fixed in the mind in the first part, the greater is the necessity of keeping clear of it in the free fantasia section. Wagner's wholesome advice to say everything in a key before leaving it has its counterpart, understood but not expressed, to avoid the same key when you have said everything in it which you want to say. Do not, therefore, discount your arrival at a given key by anticipating its entry.

(§ 14) The danger of making the keys into which you modulate sound as if they were the original key of the piece.

This may arise from two causes; either from the tonality being insufficiently driven home at the start, or from the subsidiary key being so firmly insisted on that it overbalances the original key. For this reason it is most inadvisable for a beginner to alter his key-signature in the course of a movement, as, for example, in a movement in E major, when the second subject is in B major, to alter the signature from four sharps to five. The mere sight of the original key-signature tends to keep the due balance of tonality in the mind, and to relegate every subordinate key to its proper position in the general scheme. This is one of the reasons why Brahms laid so much stress on a composer writing his clefs and key-signatures at the beginning of every page and every line. It is not waste of time to do so; the mere manual labour gives a little pause for thought, or a little rest to the brain; as a perpetual reminder of the original tonality it is invaluable. Too definite an approach to a related key may produce the same uncertainty of tonality. The modulation must be so

DANGER SIGNALS

delicately handled as to give a feeling of rest when the related key is reached without over-accentuating it. It is like paying a visit to a friend who makes you feel at home, while all the time you know that his house is not your own.

(§ 15) The danger of writing a single part in a key different from the chord last heard.

This, a most common failing, arises from the composer supplying in his own mind chords or harmonies which are not there, and, for any ears except the composer's, do not exist. The opening of Beethoven's Overture to Leonora (No. 1) is an illustration of a single part of considerable length, every note of which will conform to and combine with the opening bass note (suggesting the chord of G):

In the following bars, where he wishes to modulate

to F major, he makes his progression clear by accompanying harmonies. If, in the example given above, he had suggested after the fifth bar a modulation to D minor, instead of remaining in the key which fitted his initial note, he would have fallen into the snare thus:

His own mind could easily have supplied harmonies for such a passage, but the inexorable G in the bass of the first bar goes on sounding *in posse* all through, and would have made his modulation unintelligible to any other ear except his own. Similarly a very marked bass note, which is not clearly and logically quitted, may fog a whole passage after it; for the lowest note lasts longest in the ear, and its career must be definitely cut short before a modulation in a higher position can sound independently of it.

DANGER SIGNALS

When long passages of an *obbligato* character are written for a single instrument, such as the cor anglais solo in the third act of *Tristan*, or the unison passage in *L'Africaine*, or for a solo voice, great care must be taken to make any suggested modulations in the course of it perfectly clear from the trend of the melody itself. The following passage for the voice alone will illustrate how this can be accomplished:

The modulations at α to A major, at β to G minor, at γ through A minor to F major, and δ back to D minor are made quite clear by the "lie" of melody and by the leading notes.

(§ 16) The danger of writing *rosalias*, especially in melody.

A *rosalia* is a sequence repeated more than twice. It is the cheapest and easiest way to modulate, or to concoct a melody, but the expedient cannot be often tried without exposure of the poverty-stricken invention which takes refuge in it. None of the great tunes of the world rely on it, and only to a limited extent on sequences at all. A *rosalia* in modulation suggests at once a continuation *ad infinitum* until the phrase disappears below the bass or above the treble. In the theme of the Prometheus Variations, quoted in a former chapter, the third and fourth bars are a sequence from the first and second, but the fifth bar (after the first two notes) breaks new ground. The entr'acte to the third act of *Lohengrin* carries out the same principle. In the opening of the Prelude to *Tristan*, where there is a third repetition of the opening phrase, a rosalia is avoided by a variation. The objections to it are the sense of monotony which it invariably induces, and the lack of flow in melodic inspiration which it evidences.

(§ 17) The danger of lowering music to illustrate lower emotions and instincts.

It is not necessary, in order to depict an ugly character or a horrible situation, to illustrate it with ugly music. To do so is the worst side of bad art. Ugly music is bad music. No great painter would paint even a Caliban badly. He draws the line at characterisation. When Beethoven wrote music for one of the greatest villains in opera, Pizarro, he did not pen an ugly or even a crude bar, and yet it is a masterpiece of delineation. Nor did Weber for the characters of Lysiart and Eglantine in his *Euryanthe*. No composer of inherent nobility will so sacrifice the most noble of the arts. For music stands alone among the arts in one respect, it is incapable without association with words or action of being in itself indecent or obscene. The faults of which it can be guilty, as absolute music, are only faults of taste, not of morals. It can be vulgar and trivial, priggish and flippant, but not offensive or grossly suggestive. On the other hand, the moment action or words come into play in combination with it, it can put a magnifying glass over every detail, and can accentuate to the most appalling extent the suggestions which they give. The torture scene in Sardou's Tosca, which in itself is horrible enough, becomes ten times more so when Puccini dots the i's and crosses the t's with his vivid score. So great can be its power for good or ill that it can make a revolutionary poem egg on a mob to the wildest excesses, or a patriotic one stir a whole nation, even when the literary value of the words is of the poorest. Great and far-reaching, therefore, is the responsibility of the man who holds the musician's pen. The regulators of his work are a pure taste and a deep sense of nobility. Folk-songs are a treasure-house of both. The simple soul of the people from which they spring is often richer in both these qualities than many accomplished and versatile composers give it credit for. There is no young writer, however gifted, who can afford to ignore the lesson which they teach. They make for simplicity, for beauty, and for sincerity; and no composer who has grounded his early tastes upon them will lightly play with the fire of sensuality or vulgarity against which they are a standing protest. It is the old fight between idealism and materialism; and when music ceases to be ideal, it will abrogate its chief duty, the refinement and elevation of public taste.

(§ 18) Lastly, the danger of trying to be original.

There is nothing so dangerous to a young composer as to criticise him for lack of originality. The truest originality is, and has always been, a gradual growth and not a sudden phenomenon. Early Bach is scarcely distinguishable from Buxtehude, early Mozart from Haydn, early Beethoven from Mozart. Wagner is permeated with Weber, Brahms with Beethoven and Schubert. Their originality manifested itself as their brains developed the power of expressing themselves in a way which was personal and individual. No one dreams of calling Beethoven a plagiarist because the slow movement of his quintet for wind and piano begins like Mozart's "Batti, batti," or Brahms for starting his second Violin Sonata with the initial notes of Wagner's Preislied. The actual notes  in the first instance and  in the latter are identical, but the proof of the pudding is in the eating. They are expressed and developed in a way which is individual to the composer who wrote them. Dvořák frequently used themes which have been often heard before, but every one of them, as he handled them, were labelled with his name. Originality has far more to do with the treatment of melodies than with the invention of them. All poets and prose writers use the same vocabulary to express themselves, but it is their method of collocating words, their literary style, which shows their greater or less individuality. All painters use the same colours, but their

DANGER SIGNALS

mixing of them and their treatment and grouping of tone-values gives them their *cachet*. Efforts after premature originality will always bring mannerism in their train, and no quality in music is so ephemeral, so annoying and so irritating. It turns a philosopher into a faddist, a poet into a rhyme-jingler. A beginner must not think about originality. If he has it in his nature, it will come out as surely as the world goes round the sun. It must not be forced, or it will be insincere. Moreover, the quality of originality is so subtle and often so gradual in its process of evolution that a future generation will be in a better position to judge of its existence than a contemporary one. Every man is different from his fellows in feature, in physique and in temperament. *Ergo*, every one is to some extent original. It is only a question of degree. The only true originality is that of a man who stands midway between the average and the abnormal. Whoever has this quality will emerge without effort from the ranks of the average of his fellows, but if he is made self-conscious in the process, he will tend to enter the ranks of the abnormal. Express yourself naturally, let your imagination run, do not let yourself be worried by reminiscence hunters, say what you want to say and what you feel you must say to the best of your ability, and (except in your workmanship and technical study) with the least possible effort. You cannot conceal a commonplace idea by a contortion of forced originality. If you are going to give a new message to the world, you will do so without being conscious of it yourself. If you set out to do it consciously, you will fail because you will be trying to pose; and the man who poses is insincere. The two most vital qualities for an artist are sincerity and nobility. Without them he may gain notoriety, but will forfeit respect. With them he will take his place, be it in the lower or the higher circles of the musician's paradise, with those who have given of their best for the advancement of their art.

INDEX

Accent and quantity, 23, 24, 129–134, 143, 145, 146.
Arioso, 146.

Bach, J. S., 12, 50, 51, 52, 55, 67, 145, 150, 188.
Bass, ground, 56, 67, 68.
Bass, importance of good, 21, 34, 37, 38, 47, 50.
Beethoven, L. van, 10, 12, 25, 26–31, 37, 41–44, 52, 55, 57–63, 69, 77, 79–89, 101, 102, 108, 110, 112, 116, 120, 122, 124, 125, 146, 156, 158, 161, 169, 171, 173, 177, 183, 186, 188.
  variations analysed, 58–63.
  sonata, Op. 31, No. 1, First movement analysed, 80–88.
  sketches, 41–44.
Berlioz, H., 96, 99, 157–159, 173.
Brahms, J., 2, 10, 12, 34, 50–52, 55, 63–69, 122–125, 137.
  Haydn variations analysed, 64–69.
Bülow, Hans G. von, 23, 96, 117, 170.
Buxtehude, 188.

Canon and Fugue, 20–22.
Choral writing, 50, 127, 147–153.
Chromatics, use and abuse of, 19, 44–48, 147, 151, 152.
Climax, 38, 39, 110, 143, 177.
Colour, 74, 95–126, 136.
Compass, vocal, 134, 135, 175; instrumental, 106.

Counterpoint, strict, 3, 6–12, 50, 115, 127; modal, 12–20, 147; so-called free, 10, 11.
Cranmer, Archbishop, 138.

Dance-forms, 47, 77, 91.
Dannreuther, E., 158, 181.
Double bass, treatment of the, 105, 106, 108.
Doubling, instrumental, 107, 111, 114, 122, 142.
Dürer, Albrecht, 42.
Dunstable, John of, 142.
Dussek, 157.
Dvořák, Antonin, 77, 125, 188.

Economy of material, 9, 20, 33, 101, 108, 111, 138, 141, 163, 172, 174.
Endings of movements, 168–170.
Equal temperament, 13, 17, 147.
Expression, marks of, 117–119, 153, 154, 167.

Fantasies, or Fancies, 162, 163.
Folk-songs, 141, 142.
Form, 74–94.
Franck, César, 123.

Gluck, Chr. von, 146, 158.
Grove, Sir George, 155.

Handel, G. F., 12, 52, 133, 134, 150.
Harmony, 6–10, 21, 50, 83, 181, 183.
Hauptmann, Moritz, 23.

INDEX

Haydn, Josef, 12, 63, 77, 126, 156, 188.
Henley, W. E., 139.
Hogarth, D., 11.
Horn, treatment of the, 101–103, 107, 109, 174.

Improvising, 179, 180.
Intervals, difficult vocal, 3, 20, 127, 128, 147–152.
Intervals, ratios of, 13–17.
Italian language for musical signs, 118, 119.

Liszt, Franz, 4, 157.

Melody, 6–9; rhythmical, 25–27, 29–31; construction of, 34–48; treatment of, 49 et seq., 131–133, 183–186.
Mendelssohn-Bartholdy, F., 77, 91, 157, 161, 170.
Metronome, use of, 118, 166, 167.
Meyerbeer, G., 180, 185.
Modulation, 21, 36, 53, 57, 81 et seq., 131–133, 183–186.
Mozart, W. A., 12, 45, 101, 103–108, 110, 122, 123, 125, 146, 158, 173, 177, 188.

Nottebohm, G. von, 42.

Orchestration, 98–111, 171–177.
Originality, 76, 188, 189.

Painting, analogy of music to, 1, 2, 42, 75, 78, 93, 96, 110, 178, 186.
Palestrina, 10, 12, 13, 19, 20, 147–150, 158.
Parry, Sir Hubert, 74.
Passage-writing, 89, 129.
Plays, incidental music to, 161, 162.
Poetry, declamation of, 23, 24, 28, 129–134, 139, 140, 145, 146, 178.
Polyphony and monophony, contrast of, 83, 178.

Programme-music, 155–160, 179.
Purcell, Henry, 56, 131, 132.

Quantity and accent (see Accent).
Quartets, string, 13, 31, 44, 45, 63, 111–119, 121, 162.

Raphael Sanzio, 75, 178.
Recitative, 144–146.
Rembrandt van Rijn, 42.
Repetition, 36, 90, 91, 160.
Rests, use of, 9, 22, 47, 113, 125, 153, 170, 171.
Reynolds, Sir Joshua, 111.
Rhythm, 23; of detail, 24–27; of phrase, 27–32, 52–54, 57, 129–131; of figure, 137, 146, 167–170.
Rhythm, overlapping, 31, 54.
Rondo, 77, 78.
Rosalia, 185.
Rossini, G., 138.

Scale, pure, 13–17, 22, 114, 122, 142, 147.
Scale, whole tone, 17, 18.
Schubert, Franz, 27, 39–41, 52, 69, 77–79, 122, 125, 136–138, 140, 155, 171.
Schumann, Robert, 4, 52, 54, 61, 63, 125, 157, 162.
Shakespeare, W., 129, 178.
Sonata-form, 51, 78, 80–90.
Sonatas, 42, 79.
Songs, 33–36, 39, 69–72, 128–144.
Songs, accompaniment of, 135–138, 140–143.
Spohr, Ludwig, 46, 157.
Sterndale, Bennett W., 157.
Strauss, Johann, 10.
Strauss, Richard, 26.
Strings (see Quartet and Trio).
Symphonic poems, 157, 160.

Technique, 2, 6 et seq., 42, 51, 52; orchestral, 98 et seq., 147.
Temperament, equal, 13, 17, 147.
Tennyson, Alfred, Lord, 134, 155, 156.

INDEX

Themes, contrast of, 89.
Tonality, 36, 84, 90, 159, 160, 182, 185.
Tones, greater and lesser, 13–17.
Trios, string, 120, 121; pianoforte, 124, 125.
Tschaikowsky, P., 167.

Variations, 49–72, 141.
Verdi, G., 126, 177.
Violin, treatment of the, 4, 16, 34, 42, 55, 92, 101, 103, 104, 109, 122–125.

Violoncello, treatment of the, 106, 112, 113, 123–125.
Voice, character and treatment of the, 3, 20, 97, 98, 108, 127–154, 175, 177.
Vowels, treatment of, 135.

Wagner, Richard, 10, 12, 13, 18, 25, 26, 34–36, 45–47, 96, 99, 101–103, 108–110, 146, 158, 159, 170, 172, 173, 181, 182, 185, 186, 188.
Wiertz, 75.
Wolf, Hugo, 26.

www.ingramcontent.com/pod-product-compliance
Lightning Source LLC
Chambersburg PA
CBHW020331170426
43200CB00006B/341